Lynda Field is a trained counsellor, therapist and life coach who specializes in personal and group development. She is the author of many best-selling titles, including *Weekend Life Coach*, *60 Ways to Feel Amazing* (no. 3 on Sunday Times bestseller list) and *Self-Esteem for Women* (chosen as one of the top titles for the NHS 'Book Prescription' scheme). As well as delivering workshops and seminars worldwide she runs a popular telephone and online coaching service, and writes articles for national magazines and the press. She lives in Cambridge, UK.

Visit Lynda online at www.lyndafield.com or email her at lynda.field@btopenworld.com

By the same author

THE SELF-ESTEEM COACH

10 days to a confident new you

LYNDA FIELD

WATKINS PUBLISHING
LONDON

This edition first published in the UK and USA 2012 by
Watkins Publishing, Sixth Floor, Castle House,
75–76 Wells Street, London W1T 3QH

Design and typography copyright © Watkins Publishing 2012
Text Copyright © Lynda Field 2012

1 3 5 7 9 10 8 6 4 2

Designed and typeset by Jerry Goldie Graphic Design

Printed in China by Imago

British Library Cataloguing-in-Publication Data Available

Library of Congress Cataloging-in-Publication Data Available

ISBN: 978-1-78028-116-2

www.watkinspublishing.co.uk

Distributed in the USA and Canada by Sterling Publishing Co., Inc.
387 Park Avenue South, New York, NY 10016-8810

For information about custom editions, special sales, premium and
corporate purchases, please contact Sterling Special Sales
Department at 800-805-5489 or specialsales@sterlingpub.com

*Dedicated to the memory of Maggie Chalmers
(AKA Margarite Batease) a true Lady of the Light.
Thank you; I didn't realize just what you had
done for me.*

Contents

Acknowledgements

THANK YOU TO

My family:
Richard – my wonderful husband, man beyond compare.
Barbara and Idwal Goronwy – my parents, positive and determined.
Leilah Porter – my daughter, doing good work.
Jack Porter – my son, an uplifting spirit.
Alex Field – my son, sharing his gifts.
Alaska Porter – my granddaughter, a powerful force.
Bevan Ward – my stepson and his partner Rosie and their wonderful son Joshua, a beautiful family.

My friends:
Sue Roberts – kind and generous and always ready to listen.
Phraid Gower – determined and courageous, with a wicked sense of humour.
Pauline Pickering – walking her talk.
Conny Nowak and Ruth Bailey – my mettaful GFR buddies.

The Cambridge Sangha – a true refuge indeed.

All my other friends, colleagues and clients, too numerous to mention but all so important to me.

Michael Mann at Watkins Publishing – who gave me the break that established my career; the wheel turns and we meet again.

Shine With Self-Esteem

When your life looks like a mountain, impossible to climb, don't ever forget how incredible you are.
You have all the resources you need to see you through.

The impression you convey is an expression of yourself that depends upon your innermost thoughts and feelings.
And when you walk in your confident shoes your bright spirit will always attract success.

Your originality and special flair make you fabulous, glorious and amazing, so love the skin you are in and know your true worth, every single day.

Each time you strive to be your highest self you are an inspiration to all those around you; be glad to let your light shine.
Your inner conviction and love for life will see you through the difficult times and even in your darkest moments this light within will sustain you.

Self-belief gives you the will to reach for your best and succeed whatever the circumstances. The past has no power over you; you can make new confident choices in the present moment – now!

Introduction

Because You Are Worth It

I wanted to become famous to prove I was a worthy person, but eventually I realized only you can make yourself feel worthy.

Davina McCall (television presenter)

Self-esteem is a vital ingredient for personal success and happiness. When we have it we feel good about ourselves; we are calm, confident and in control and everything seems possible. Don't you just love it when you feel like this?

But our self-esteem is rather like a fragile flower; it bruises easily and needs lots of nurturing and tender loving care. Even the most seemingly confident people have to work on maintaining their self-worth, although you might find this hard to believe. When our self-esteem is low, it is only too easy to imagine that everyone else in the world is brimming with confidence and positivity. But this is an illusion; at times we all struggle with issues of self-doubt and negativity. My clients come from all walks of life and I assure you that the rich, the famous and the beautiful can have as many self-esteem issues as the rest of us.

We are inclined to think that worldly success automatically brings self-esteem, but this is not necessarily true. Although it's great to do well we cannot rely on our achievements to make us feel valuable and worthy enough to be here. Favourable circumstances can change, life brings inevitable challenges and when things don't look so hot for us we have to rely on our personal inner strengths to see us through. *The Self-Esteem Coach* shows you just how to activate and build these essential inner qualities. Whenever we are feeling not so good, our self-esteem drops, we stop believing in ourselves and we fail to remember that we are a walking miracle. And once we lose our strong sense of self-worth we can easily forget our inner brilliance and fall headlong into a downbeat cycle of self-doubt and increasing negativity. But take heart, because this means that if you think that low self-worth lies at the root of your personal problems then you can change the quality of your life by working directly on activating and increasing your self-esteem.

Sometimes it may only take a small gesture or action to change your mood to a more positive state: a kind word from a colleague, the smile of a stranger, a walk in the park, a new lipstick, a call to a friend, a cupcake ... But at other times you might need something more and that is why I wrote *The Self-Esteem Coach: 10 Days to a Confident New You*. This 10-day self-esteem programme is a simple step-by-step approach to regaining your naturally confident, balanced and motivated self. Combining theory and practice with a fresh modern take, it is grounded in the scientifically acclaimed disciplines of cognitive behavioural therapy (CBT) and positive psychology, and includes practical ideas, techniques and strategies from recognized spiritual traditions, cosmic ordering, neuro-linguistic programming (NLP) and up-to-the minute counselling and coaching theory.

The fundamental quality of our lives reflects our innermost thoughts, feelings, beliefs, expectations and imaginings. Our thoughts are powerful manifesters of reality as they connect and give rise to our emotions and to our actions. Although we can consider our thoughts, feelings and behaviour independently they are actually closely inter-related – a change in any one of these factors will have an immediate effect on the other two. Figure 1 uses a cognitive behavioural therapy model to demonstrate the interconnectedness and interdependency of the thoughts, feelings and behaviour of a person with high self-

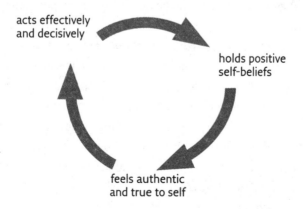

Figure 1: A Person with High Self-Esteem

esteem. I love the clear way that CBT demonstrates our potential for self-transformation by showing us that a small change in the way we think, feel or act can have a radical effect on our experience.

Self-esteem does not depend on success but success naturally comes to those with self-esteem. And when our self-worth is low, life seems full of setbacks and difficulties. So exactly how does this work; how do our self-doubts limit our experiences and close the doors to opportunity and happiness? I expect that you know the answers to these questions only too well. Consider any recent occasion where your feelings of not being quite 'good enough' scuppered your success. Look back at the incident and relive the experience – what were your thoughts about yourself, how were you feeling and how did you act? Now try re-running that old 'failure' scenario, changing the key elements as you go. This time you are self-supporting and validating, believing that you are an intrinsically worthy person who deserves success. Notice how your feelings about yourself match your thoughts exactly – you feel confident and authentic. And the consequences of your positive thoughts and emotions naturally give rise to creative and effective behaviour. Lo and behold you have instantly become a mover and a shaker in your own life. Sounds like a dream? Start now to visualize this confident new you and begin to make that dream come true.

Psychologist Nathaniel Branden defines self-esteem as, 'confidence in our ability to think, confidence in our ability to cope with the basic challenges of life, and confidence in our right to be successful and happy, the feeling of being worthy, deserving, entitled to assert our needs and wants, achieve our values, and enjoy the fruits of our effort'.

Take a few moments to think about how this definition relates to you. Consider each of the issues mentioned, which are listed below, and give yourself a rating from 1 to 10 (with 1 being the lowest score and 10 the highest).

TOPIC	RATING
Level of clarity of my thinking	
My ability to cope with basic challenges	
Belief in my right to be successful and happy	
Level of feelings of deservability and worthiness	
Belief in my right to assert my needs and wants	
Level of feelings of entitlement to enjoy the rewards of my effort	

Make a note of your answers and any feelings that arise as you do this exercise.

We will be returning to these issues later in the book to consider them in greater detail. Now might be a good time to buy a beautiful spiral-bound notebook and begin your own self-esteem journal; this will enable you to keep track of your ongoing thoughts and reflections. As you go through the programme you will start to become more and more aware of the ways that your thoughts, feelings and behaviour are affecting your levels of self-value and self-worth. These personal revelations will make it increasingly easy for you to pinpoint the changes that you need to make to increase your self-esteem.

How the 10-Day Self-Esteem Programme Works

Of course we all want to feel good about ourselves and our world. We want to: be happy and relaxed; have great relationships; attract prosperity and success; be motivated and enthusiastic; live a meaningful life and feel in control of our destiny. But where to begin? I know from long experience that anyone can change their life for the better, but they can only do so if they are in possession of three magical elements. When you bought this book you demonstrated two of the qualities that are absolutely necessary for your success: a strong *intention to change* and an *unshakeable belief* that this is possible. The third requirement is an *excellent and foolproof plan*! I have designed the programme to fit in with any lifestyle. Each day introduces a new topic and so you can dip in and out as time allows or you can begin at the beginning and follow the programme for 10 days.

Let *The Self-Esteem Coach* be an interactive experience for you. You bring your own unique self to the table and we all see things quite differently so be prepared to work creatively with the ideas in this book. Use your journal to jot down your answers to the exercises and also to add your own ideas, responses, thoughts and reflections. Question and investigate your process thoroughly – be your own coach. When you use the book like this it will become a meaningful reflection of your deepest beliefs, thoughts, feelings and desires. It will provide a personal record of your levels of self-esteem and it will demonstrate easy-to-use, practical techniques that you can apply to make changes in all areas of your life. You will create a confident new you who can finally bring your dreams into reality.

In my long career I have been privileged to hear many hundreds of wonderful stories of self-transformation. The most powerful positive changes often occur in the face of the greatest adversity so never ever give up on yourself. Fill your life with self-esteem and enjoy your full potential by discovering your own incredible and unique creative spirit.

You *can* change your life around, you have what it takes; begin today!

Part One

Take Control

Day 1

Choose High Self-Esteem

I'm just like everyone else – I have days when I feel great and days when I don't feel so good. I'm not a terminally confident person, I'm really not.

Helen Mirren (actress)

I can see, hear, think, say and do.

I have the tools to survive, to be close to others, to be productive, and to make sense and order out of the world of people and things outside of me.

I own me, and therefore I can engineer me.

I am me and I am okay.

Virginia Satir (psychotherapist)

And this is exactly the right place to start; recognizing that you are you and that you are okay. Your sense of self-esteem is embedded in your self-belief, so let 'I am OK' become a guiding principle for you, whatever is going on. For example, if you make a mistake or let yourself down in some way it is only too easy to beat yourself up about it and then to descend into a downward self-critical spiral leading to feelings of abject misery and worthlessness. At such a time it is good to remember that you are okay and that you have only made a mistake. People with self-esteem can allow themselves not to be perfect and still be OK.

You also own yourself and therefore can 'engineer' yourself. In other words, because you know yourself intimately you actually already know exactly what you need to do to realize your greatest potential. When coaching clients, they sometimes say that they are amazed by what I seem to know about them, but I can only ever know what they have already revealed to me. You really do know yourself very well but you just might have forgotten how special, worthy and lovable you are.

Because we are human we are always in the process of learning about ourselves and our world, and so we are inevitably facing new challenges all the time. Our biggest challenge will always be *to remember that we are special, worthy and lovable*, however difficult life may be sometimes. I love the way that Helen Mirren describes herself as not being 'terminally confident'; she may be a supremely talented, successful and gorgeous woman but she still has days when her confidence dips – we all do! Our self-esteem is ultra sensitive to pervading conditions; our feelings about ourselves can change dramatically from day to day, indeed from moment to moment. Check how you are feeling about yourself right now.

Initial Self-Esteem Checklist

	agree	disagree
I am optimistic		
I make good decisions		
It's OK to be angry		
I believe in me		
I trust my intuition		
The world is a beautiful place		
It's OK for me to make mistakes		
I love and value myself		
I can allow myself to feel sad		

	agree	disagree
I believe that I can change	|
I can forgive myself	|
I can say 'no' when I need to	|
I express my feelings easily	|
I deserve the best that life has to offer	|

How did you answer these questions? Are you feeling powerful, confident, decisive and at one with the world, or are you feeling threatened, insecure and out of control? In other words, are you feeling high or low in self-esteem?

What is Self-Esteem?

Listed below are some of the things that people have associated with having high or low self-esteem.

high self-esteem	low self-esteem
Vitality	Lethargy
Having confidence	Lacking confidence
Feeling happy	Feeling unhappy
Being relaxed	Being uptight
Security	Insecurity
Peaceful and calm	Stretched and stressed

high self-esteem cont.	**low self-esteem** cont.
Dignity	Shame
Realistic expectations	Unrealistic expectations
Good personal boundaries	Poor personal boundaries
In control	Out of control
Feeling 'in the flow'	Feeling stuck
Success	Failure
Charismatic personality	Weak personality
Feeling authentic	Feeling like a fraud
Self-respect	No self-respect
Work/life balance	Burnout
Enthusiasm	Depression
Feeling connected	Feeling isolated

How do you relate to these ideas? Do you disagree with any of them? Have you anything you would like to add to these lists?

. . . .

. . . .

. . . .

Today we begin this programme by committing ourselves to choosing to have high self-esteem rather than low self-esteem. I imagine that you might be wondering if this can be an issue of choice. When self-doubt rears its ugly head and we bow to the apparently inevitable feelings of powerlessness and failure, it can be hard to believe we don't have to take this route. People are inclined to think that high self-esteem is a quality that you have or you don't. In my practice I often hear clients say that they can't do something or other because their self-esteem is too low, perhaps you have said or thought this in the past. But when we take a closer look at the phenomenon of self-esteem we see that it is affected by certain conditions and that it is in fact possible to change these conditions.

How We Experience High and Low Self-Esteem

Self-belief is at the very heart of self-esteem. If I believe that I am 'not good enough', worthless and incapable, then my *feelings* about myself will reflect these *thoughts*. My *behaviour* will reflect my low opinion and so my total experience will be one of low self-esteem. Whenever we blame and criticize ourselves our *behaviour* will always be ineffective.

However, if my *thoughts* about myself are encouraging and supportive and I believe that I am intrinsically a worthy person who deserves self-respect, then my *feelings* about myself will be upbeat and authentic and I will act effectively – I will be able to make great things happen in my life. Our self-beliefs or *thoughts* about ourselves have an immediate effect on our *feelings* and our *behaviour*.

To each experience we bring our whole self, that is to say we integrate our mind, body, spirit and emotions. This means that our *thoughts, feelings* and *behaviour* exist simultaneously; they are inter-related and in fact create each other to give rise to our total experience. *See* figure 2.

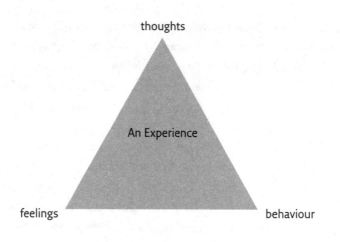

Figure 2: A Total Experience

Let's see how this might work in real life.

Example 1: Imagine that you have just been offered a long-awaited promotion at work. Of course you would be uplifted by the news with accompanying positive thoughts such as: *I am good at what I do, I deserve this post, my colleagues appreciate my skills* … etc. Naturally you will feel an increase in wellbeing and purposefulness, which will automatically lead to more focused, assertive and decisive behaviour. You will enjoy an experience of high self-esteem.

Example 2: And now imagine that the longed-for promotion went to someone else. How do you think you would feel? Well you always have a choice about the way you see things. It would be only too easy to get into a deeply negative state over this by thinking, *I'm not good enough, people don't like me, I'll never get a better job* … etc. Such thoughts would lead to feelings of hopelessness and low confidence and you would soon begin to act like a victim.

It is natural to be disillusioned when we feel let down by life, but people with high self-esteem work consistently to ensure that disappointments and setbacks don't plunge them into a state of insecurity and lack of self-belief. The main point here is that, as far as self-confidence is concerned, attitude is everything! Of course it is relatively easy to feel buoyant when things are going along swimmingly. But we all know that life brings us new challenges on a daily basis and we either rise to face them or sink under the pressure. Everything changes and we must change too; sometimes the stress of this can overwhelm us and make us feel insecure, threatened and vulnerable. Our thoughts, feelings and behaviour are constantly in flux (focus on your mind chatter for a moment and you will see how true this is) and so this means that our levels of self-esteem can easily alter from one moment to the next. You will know only too well how a blow to your confidence can have swift and far-reaching effects on your mood. It only takes someone to press one of our 'vulnerable' buttons and off we can go down that slippery slope of negativity into self-doubt, which leads directly into victim-like behaviour. And I know that this happens to you because it happens to all of us.

Take strength from the fact that *everyone's* feelings of self-worth go up and down. Perhaps this might help you to feel kinder and more loving to yourself. You are not alone in your insecurities and self-doubts, they are perfectly natural and they don't need to ruin your life, which you will see as you work through this book. My experience with clients demonstrates that once we can let ourselves off the hook, even a little bit, we can begin to stop the unending self-criticism and start to appreciate ourselves. This is most important because we will never be able to value the gift of our life if we cannot value ourselves.

CONFIDENCE TIP
Value Your Success

You are a fabulous person and you have unique strengths and talents, even if you do not always appreciate them. Many of us are inclined to be continually moving the goalposts and this does us a great disservice. Just when we are about to achieve a success it becomes 'not quite enough' and we demand even more of ourselves. Because we hardly ever celebrate our successes, they just get lost along the way.

- Notice when an achievement is 'not enough' in itself.

- Consider why you might feel the need to keep 'proving yourself' to yourself and others.

- Begin to value each and every one of your successes, however small they may seem.

- Give yourself a pat on the back for all your efforts.

- Appreciate yourself – you are doing your best!

Thoughts, Feelings and Behaviour that Create High or Low Self-Esteem

Listed below are various psychological, emotional and behavioural states that are associated with having high and low self-esteem.

A Person With High Self-Esteem Thinks	A Person With Low Self-Esteem Thinks
I believe in myself	I can't believe in myself
I deserve the best	I am undeserving
I trust my instincts	I can't trust my instincts
I am in control	I have lost control
I value myself	I have no self-respect
I can change	I cannot change
I am a success	I am a failure
I can make things happen	I am ineffective
I am good enough	I am not good enough
I do the best I can	I fall short of my expectations

Feels	Feels
Spontaneous	Uptight and rigid
Optimistic	Pessimistic
Positive	Negative
Free of guilt	Guilty
Appreciated	Criticized
Supported	Victimized

Kindness towards others	Antisocial
Motivated	Unmotivated
Balanced	Out of sorts
Relaxed	Worried

Behaves	**Behaves**
Effectively	Ineffectively
Openly	Defensively
Can say no	Can't say no
Creatively	Unimaginatively
Can take risks	Can't take risks
Trustingly	Fearfully
Can show emotion	Can't show emotion
Lovingly	Critically
Light-heartedly	Despondently
Assertively	Passive/aggressively

Can you add anything to these lists?

. . . .

. . . .

Can you see how these various states contribute to creating either high or low self-esteem?

Our thoughts, feelings and behaviour are always changing and our levels of self-esteem can alter from one minute to the next. You may be swinging along full of positive self-beliefs, feeling great and then ... something happens. This 'something' can be any circumstance which knocks you off your even keel by encouraging self-criticism. And so, the thoughts that were supporting your high self-esteem can change. If this happens you will suddenly find yourself sinking into a whirlpool of your negative self-beliefs. Instead of believing that you deserve the best and feeling in control of your life, you will now believe that you are worthless and powerless – you have become a victim of circumstances! The speed at which this change can happen is really quite frightening. As soon as the quality of your thoughts changes, your feelings and behaviour correspond exactly. Instead of feeling optimistic and relaxed, you will now feel insecure and will be acting ineffectively and indecisively.

Your thoughts create the quality of your experience, so become aware of what you are thinking. When you choose to be positive your confidence grows.

EXERCISE

When Your High Self-Esteem Changed to Low Self-Esteem

Think of a time when you felt high in self-esteem and then something occurred which totally demoralized you. Perhaps someone criticized you in a particularly sensitive area; maybe you felt that you were shamed in some way or that you simply could not cope. Try to reconstruct the exact circumstances surrounding this situation.

1 Describe how you were thinking about yourself when you were high in self-esteem, before the event occurred.

. . . .

. . . .

. . . .

2 What was your emotional state at this time?

. . . .

. . . .

. . . .

. . . .

3 How were you acting before the event?

. . . .

. . . .

. . . .

. . . .

Now recreate the sensations that were linked with losing your self-esteem.

4 What were you thinking about yourself after the event?

. . . .

. . . .

. . . .

. . . .

5 What mood do you associate with your loss of self-esteem at this time?

....

....

....

6 How did your behaviour change after the event had occurred?

....

....

....

It seems as though our self-esteem is always on the line. We can go up and down and up and down again with alarming speed. Does this sound like you?

_____

If you feel criticized by others your self-doubts will surface. Don't let yourself be affected by the opinion of other people.

EXERCISE

The Cycle of Transformation

The interdependency of our beliefs (thoughts), feelings (moods) and behaviour (actions) means that if we consciously change any one of these three then we can transform the nature of our experience. Let's see how this works.

Review your answers to the previous exercise. Notice the particular relationship between your thoughts, moods and actions before and then after the situation which took you from high to low self-esteem. It is possible to change the effects of this process – you can recover your self-esteem! Figure 3 (page 18) 'The cycle of transformation', shows how easy it is to do this.

Take your answers to questions 4, 5 and 6 and insert them in the appropriate places in Figure 3(a). Describe your disheartening event in the space provided. Now look at your completed Figure 3(a).

What does it show you about the relationship between your thoughts, mood and actions on this occasion? Do these elements create a chain reaction? Do they seem to give rise to each other?

Think about the answers you have inserted in the figure. Which, if any, of those reactions could you change?

Could you alter your thoughts about this situation? For example, would you have been so flattened if you had been able to maintain a strong belief about yourself, in spite of the circumstances?

Could you change the way you feel about the event? For example, would it have been possible to bring some humour into the situation, would that have lightened your mood?

Would it be possible to act differently? Maybe you didn't say what you really meant.

Figure 3: The Cycle of Transformation

3(a)

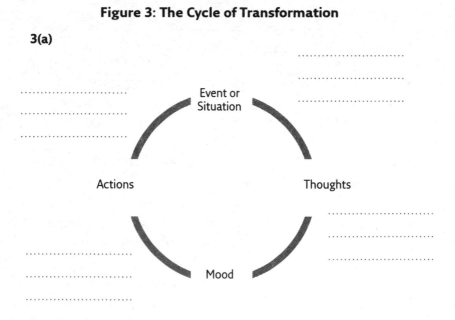

3(b)

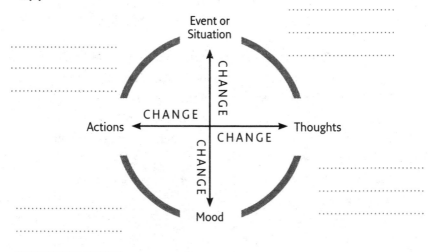

Reflect on the event, thoughts, feelings and actions that cost you your self-esteem. There is always so much scope for us to change unless we want to stay stuck for some reason. The cycle of transformation is a really useful tool for helping us to understand our reactions to certain conditions and to see how we could cope differently and maintain our self-esteem.

Think of one reaction that you could change. Insert this in the appropriate space in Figure 3(b).

How does this change the other elements in Figure 3(b)?

Now you have changed one response in the diagram, fill in the other spaces. Has everything changed? Has this response altered your perception of the initial event in some way? Be as inventive as you can and feel free to use your imagination to create a completely different scenario. Next time a similar situation arises could you maintain your self-esteem?

You could draw your own transformation cycles and use them whenever you are looking low self-esteem in the eye. Be creative: remember you can always change. If your reactions can create low self-worth then they can also create high self-worth. Always choose responses that support your self-esteem.

INSIGHT

Your Future Is Bright

You know that you can change, if you didn't know this to be true then you wouldn't be reading this book. And it is your belief in self-transformation that secures your bright future.

Look at the following possibilities.

You can:

- Change your beliefs about yourself

- Alter your mood

- Act differently

- Decide to value and appreciate yourself

- Become a 'can do' person

- Adopt an optimistic approach

- Begin a new adventure

- Smile in the face of adversity

- Allow yourself to be less than perfect

- Believe that you can be a success

- Leave negativity behind

- Know your intrinsic worthiness

- Keep confident in the face of challenges

Consider this: *Although you might believe something negative about yourself it doesn't necessarily mean that it is true.*

Case Study

Sophie, 33, is the photography manager for a London-based online designer clothing and accessories retailer. A rising star in the fashion industry, with a smart flat in Pimlico and a large social circle, Sophie certainly appeared to 'have it all'. We met when I gave a talk on inner style and confidence at the Clothes Show Live in Birmingham and we exchanged cards. A few months later she rang me for coaching for what she called her 'secret insecurity issue'. Sophie is lovely, talented and gregarious but deep inside she was struggling to live up to her image. She said that her successes often brought with them mixed feelings of anxiety and doubt about her ability to live up to her own reputation. When I asked her to explain this a bit more she said that she spent a lot of time 'feeling like a fraud who is going to be found out soon'. She admitted that she was good at what she did and that her feelings were actually quite illogical.

We often find that there is actually very little evidence to support our limiting self-beliefs and we can see that our negative emotions are not really founded in logic. Emotions are irrational and it is good to remember this whenever you find yourself losing self-belief for no obvious reason. What we do know from CBT is that it is possible to trace an emotion back to the thoughts that gave rise to it, and that if we change the nature of the thought we can change the nature of the emotion. I used this technique with Sophie and she spent the first four weeks of coaching recognizing her own negative thought processes, documenting them and discussing their reality quotient with me. I asked her to mentally 'catch' any negative thought about herself as she was thinking it and then to ask herself, 'but is this really true?'. This is such a great technique because it begins to shine a light on the many self-critical thoughts that we habitually repeat day in and day out.

Sophie was horrified to discover how many times a day she thought something that she did or said was 'not good enough'. On deeper reflection she realized that she had always wanted things to be 'perfect' from a very early age. This 'quest for perfection' is a common theme amongst women and means that achievement comes at a high price – *dissatisfaction with self, however well we have done!* Sophie eventually traced her perfectionist tendencies right back to being a toddler when she started trying to please her father who was a highly critical man. As all this awareness unravelled, Sophie began to gain a new perspective on her thinking and eventually was able to accept that whatever she did was actually quite 'good enough'.

Self-change is not so hard. By simply 'watching' the exact ways that you think, feel and behave, you will start to develop a new, kinder and more accepting understanding towards yourself.

The Power of Self-Kindness

If self-esteem was a flower then where would we find its roots? This may be easier to answer if we first consider the roots of low self-esteem. We know that its origins lie in lack of self-worth, little confidence and no feeling of intrinsic value. But I want us to go further back, behind even these characteristics, and when we do this we come to what I think of as *the seed of low self-esteem: lack of kindness to self.* We know how self-belief naturally leads to high esteem, but how can we trust and believe in someone who we don't like and appreciate? If we are unkind to ourselves we will stay stuck in a negative place leading downhill fast!

We are so excellent at being kind to others, doing good deeds and looking out for our friends and family, but we all struggle with showing love and compassion to ourselves. The unkindness that we bestow upon ourselves can surpass anything that others may possibly inflict upon us. That oh so familiar, critical inner voice telling you that you are *useless, no good, not clever/thin/beautiful enough, hopeless* ... etc. knows exactly how to keep punishing you with its relentless cruelty. Just as you are about to take that exciting new leap it whispers such things as: *who do you think you are, you are never going to be a success, you don't deserve this, oh just give up before you make a fool of yourself* ... etc. Later on we will take a long hard look at this voice: what it says, how it says it and why it began speaking to you in this unhelpful and discouraging way. For now we are simply recognizing that it is unkind and hurtful; if we believe what it says we will always be low in self-esteem.

The Buddha said that: 'You can search throughout the entire universe for someone who is more deserving of your love and affection than you are yourself, and that person is not to be found anywhere. You yourself, as much as anybody in the entire universe deserve your love and affection.' How do you react to this statement? What would it mean to love yourself more? Can you let yourself believe that you deserve all the love and kindness you can get? How could you give yourself more affection?

10 Ways to be Kinder to Yourself

1 *Stop focusing on what you can't do* and start focusing on what you can do. Changing the direction of your attention in this way will certainly uplift your spirits.

2 *Buy yourself a beautiful bunch of flowers*, some delicious fruit, your favourite magazine ... just because you deserve a treat.

3 *Don't worry about what people think* – unsurprisingly, everyone else is pretty much taken up with themselves and is unlikely to be judging you.

4 *Count your blessings.* Michael McCullough, a psychology professor at the University of Miami says that, 'Grateful people are happier, more optimistic, more satisfied with their lives ...'

5 *Smile and spread those good vibrations.* Yes, you can do this, and when you do you will attract new, positive, life affirming energy.

6 *Do something you love*: take a walk in the park, curl up with a new novel, meet up with a friend, go for a swim ...

7 *Talk nicely to yourself.* Let your self-talk be encouraging and helpful. Abandon self-criticism for a day and see what a difference this makes to your mood.

8 *Stop striving to be permanently confident.* This is probably the most effective tip in the book. You will never stay unaffected by life's ups and downs but know that you can always bounce back.

9 *Give yourself time to make decisions*, you don't have to react immediately to the suggestions of others.

10 *Be yourself.* This means letting yourself be who you are and not who you think you 'should' be.

There are of course many ways to be kinder to ourselves and as you work through this book you will uncover more and more of them. Your growing self-knowledge acts like a giant laser beam scanning your psyche and alighting upon patterns of self-doubt and self-dislike that you might never have noticed before. This amazing process will enable you to see the *exact* nature of the repetitive negative patterns that lead to your feelings of low self-esteem and lack of confidence. Use your growing self-awareness to help you observe any unkind thoughts you have about yourself; any feelings of self-criticism that may arise, and any hurtful behaviours that you might inflict upon yourself. And when you notice any unhelpful patterns try not to berate yourself even more, but adopt the self-kindness habit instead. Simply ask yourself this question, 'How could I be kinder to myself right now?' and then follow your own good advice.

Day 1 | Review

The confident new you is bursting to emerge, but will not be able to do so until you start to activate the ideas we are discussing. At the end of each day there will be a summary of the key issues and an opportunity to create your own personal self-esteem action plan. This is where your journal will be useful. I suggest that you make notes on anything that arises for you as you are working through the 10-day programme, and then take a look at them at the end of the day when you reach the Review. Consider the key reflections and anything else that has made an impact on you. Be prepared for unusual insights at any time. When you are working on yourself at this deep level you might have meaningful dreams, vivid recollections of the past, or sudden realizations that seem to occur from out of the blue. Keep note of anything that is significant.

Key Reflections for Day 1

- High or low self-esteem, the choice is always yours.
- Your biggest challenge will always be to remember that you are special, worthy and lovable even when you are not feeling so good about yourself.
- Your thoughts, feelings and behaviour are constantly changing and this means that your levels of self-esteem can easily alter from one moment to the next.
- Everyone's feelings of self-worth and confidence are continually rising and falling.
- People with high self-esteem work consistently to ensure that personal setbacks don't plunge them into the depths of insecurity and self-doubt.
- It is important to value every one of your successes, however small they might seem – self-appreciation boosts your confidence.

- The quality of each of your experiences will depend upon the exact nature of your thoughts, feelings and behaviour.
- If your reactions can create low self-worth then they can also create high self-worth.
- You know that you can change, and this belief secures your bright future.
- Although you might believe something negative about yourself it doesn't necessarily mean that it is true.
- Lack of kindness to self is the seed that grows low self-esteem. Plant the kindness seed and watch yourself blossom.

Your 3-Point Action Plan for Day 1

This is where you can begin to put into practice some of the things we have been looking at.

1 Take any insight that you have made today:
  Example: *I hate myself whenever I think I have made a mistake.*

2 Consider the patterns (thought/emotional/behavioural) that might lie behind this:
  Example: *I am only satisfied if I think I am right/perfect even!*

3 Create an action point around a possible change of response:
  Example: *I will start noticing each time I have to be right and remind myself that we all make mistakes.*

Try this 3-point action plan for yourself.

My personal insights:

. . . .

. . . .

The patterns that might lie behind this:

. . . .

. . . .

My action points:

. . . .

. . . .

This simple structure can be used to create a practical application from any personal insight that you have. We will use this technique over and over again as you start breaking the negative habits that take away your happiness and confidence.

Day 2

Think Positively

There is not much upside in self-doubt.

Hugh Hendry (hedge-fund manager)

A man is largely what he thinks about all day long.

Ralph Waldo Emerson (philosopher and poet)

When I arrived at York University in 1971, to read Social Sciences, I was rather hoping that by studying psychology and sociology I would find the answers to some big pressing questions. To borrow from Douglas Adams' *The Hitchhiker's Guide to the Galaxy*, I was after the 'ultimate answer to the ultimate question of life, the universe, and everything'. I have to report that my progress in this area has been slow, but on the other hand my deep desire to understand the process of self-transformation has led to a wonderful and fascinating career.

It has often been said that we only really learn about ourselves when we have to dig deep in the face of life's challenges and this has always been true for me, personally. When I was 33, a single parent with two very young children, I lost my optimistic spirit and couldn't find it anywhere. Up until then, life had been going fairly well and I was busy being married and having babies and not really thinking about the state of my psyche. While things run smoothly we are inclined to just get on and enjoy our lives but of course this state never lasts, everything changes and sometimes we don't like the change. My marriage ended; I moved to Bristol with my children and it felt like my life had turned upside down. Naturally I wanted to change how I felt, and to my dismay I discovered that I *still* didn't have a clue about how to start; and this is where my real quest for self-transformation began. Needs must, as they say, and so my fascination with self-change was ignited by the simple fact that I had to do something to save myself! Just when things were getting very desperate and I began hitting the vodka bottle far too often, I came across Louise Hay's book *You Can Heal Your Life*. Of course this was 25 years ago when the self-help genre was in its infancy. Her book introduced me to two radical ideas which changed my life completely and I think still remain central to any successful personal development programme. The following two quotes are taken from *You Can Heal Your Life*.

Radical Idea 1

> *Because we choose all of our thoughts we can change them.*

'Believe it or not, we do choose our thoughts. We may habitually think the same thought over and over so that it does not seem we are choosing the thought. But we did make the original choice. We can refuse to think certain thoughts. Look how often you have refused to think a positive thought about yourself. Well you can also refuse to think a negative thought about yourself.'

I had never read anything like this before and it opened up my life again. Although this might seem fairly unoriginal now when so many people have such a sophisticated knowledge of CBT, positive psychology, NLP and the rest, it is good to remember that self-change *always* involves this very basic understanding: we choose what we believe to be true.

Radical Idea 2

> *Lack of self-worth is simply another expression of not loving ourselves.*

'I never believe it when clients try to convince me how terrible they are, or how unlovable they are. My work is to bring them back to the time when they knew how to really love themselves.'

All those years ago when I was full of anger and guilt and self-dislike, I remember crying when I read this. How amazing that bringing people back to feeling good about themselves eventually became my work too!

Many of you, I know, have done a lot of personal development work, have read numerous books on the subject, maybe attended workshops and possibly had therapy of some kind. You know that the process of self-change is usually a gradual one and that this path requires persistence, determination, stamina and a large dose of self-acceptance. It is certainly a paradox, that we can begin to change only when we can appreciate how we are right now (warts and all). The reason for this is that as soon as we stop being kind to ourselves we become stuck in a cul-de-sac from which it is hard to escape.

self-criticism → self-doubt → feelings of helplessness → inability to affect change → even more self-criticism ...

To break free of this bleak cycle we need to give ourselves a bit of a hug or even a great big hug. Sometimes when I feel myself approaching this punishing cycle I actually cross my arms over my chest and give myself a cuddle – it acts as a reminder and a warning to stop that unkind thought right now, or else I will be in big trouble. Why not try this, next time you sense that a self-critical thought is hovering in your consciousness? Even if you only manage to do this occasionally you will be starting to break a longstanding habit that only serves to lower your self-esteem.

CONFIDENCE TIP

Simply Witness any Negative Thoughts

Witnessing your thoughts means just that. You notice a negative self-belief (*oh I can't do that, I am utterly hopeless, why can't I be as good as ..., if only I wasn't so ..., I am so stupid ...*) and you remain dispassionate. Just observe the thought without adding to its weight. In other words, retain your objectivity by being aware of the negativity without giving yourself extra grief by further criticism. Self-awareness is a powerful tool for self-change, and sometimes becoming aware of a bad mental habit is all we need in order to change. However, you might be surprised to notice that the first flash of self-awareness is quickly followed by another thought which will be making a judgement of some sort (*that is so negative, there I am at it again bringing myself down, when I am going to stop doing this ...*). Witness this too and remain detached, otherwise you can see where this is going to take you. For example:

1 I notice myself getting panicky in a social setting.

2 I tell myself that I am just *too shy* and that I must get a grip.

3 I witness this and then I have a split-second choice: to be angry with myself even further (and compound the panic) or to just witness this also.

Witnessing creates some space and freedom for us when we are looking at our negativity. It gives us the chance to stop being totally reactive to our thoughts, feelings and emotions. Instead of becoming completely overwhelmed, we can watch, observe, and then maybe even find some compassion for ourselves.

What Do You Believe About Yourself?

Our thoughts create our reality, and our self-esteem rises and falls in direct correlation with our self-belief. So any discussion of self-esteem must include an evaluation of our self-beliefs. Take a look at Figure 4.

We know that the quality of our self-belief directly affects our levels of self-esteem. With strong self-belief we have the confidence to climb every mountain; nothing whatsoever can stand in our way. And when we lose those good thoughts about ourselves, those mountains become bigger, more frightening and impossible to scale. We also know that we can change our beliefs – what amazingly good news this is! But before we can change any beliefs that might be causing us grief, we need to know exactly what they are and this is not always obvious. We might be so used to talking ourselves down that we don't even realize we are doing it. Try the following exercise which will reveal exactly what you believe to be true about yourself.

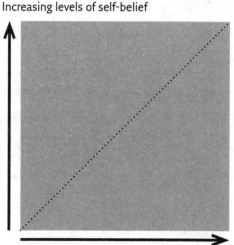

Figure 4: The Relationship between Self-Esteem and Self-Belief

Self-Image Questionnaire

Step 1 What do think you are like? How do you see yourself? What do you think are your strengths and weaknesses? Put *I am* before each word and score as shown:

0 hardly ever **1** occasionally **2** frequently **3** nearly always

anxious	persistent	creative	aggressive
intuitive	embarrassed	controlling	enthusiastic
guilty	forgiving	suspicious	caring
upbeat	dutiful	tactful	sensitive
happy	passive	patient	empathetic
spontaneous	organized	decisive	stupid
thoughtful	responsible	flexible	emotional
gullible	reliable	sociable	interesting
self-effacing	kind	energetic	introverted
noisy	intense	engaged	charismatic
dull	openhearted	miserable	motivated
fearful	dependent	gentle	powerless
friendly	clever	adaptable	open
moralistic	overbearing	funny	tollerant
logical	self-conscious	uptight	inspired
optimistic	courageous	addicted	insensitive

Step 2 Which adjectives scored 3? In other words what do you think you are nearly always?

I am nearly always:

. . . .

. . . .

These defining features are part of your self-image. How do you think these aspects of your personality increase or decrease your level of self-esteem.

. . . .

. . . .

If, for example, you think that you are nearly always *optimistic*, then this will enhance your image and uplift your vision of yourself and the world. If you believe that your cup is half full, rather than half empty, then you will attract powerful positive energy into your life; others will respond to your personal magnetism and all your relationships will improve dramatically. On the other hand, if you believe that you are nearly always *powerless* then you will be inclined to let others walk all over you and this will only drag you down even lower.

Reflect on where you scored 3 and ask yourself whether these characteristics serve to increase or decrease your self-esteem. Remember that just because you believe something about yourself it does not necessarily mean that it is true. If one of your self-beliefs is making you miserable then you have the power to change it, and once you change a thought you will immediately affect the way you feel and act. Which, if any, of these characteristics would you like to change?

. . . .

. . . .

Step 3 Where did you score 0? What do you think you are hardly ever?

I am hardly ever:

. . . .

. . . .

Your self-image does not include these personality traits. How does the apparent lack of these features affect your self-esteem?

. . . .

. . . .

. . . .

For example, if you consider that you are hardly ever uptight then this would contribute to a high level of self-esteem. But if you scored 0 for decisive you would demonstrate a lack of clarity that would undermine your ability to take positive action, and this would certainly create feelings of low self-esteem.

Which, if any, of these characteristics would you like to change?

. . . .

. . . .

Step 4 List eight adjectives that best describe you. Take words from my list or use your own.

I am:

. . . .

Choose the adjective that encapsulates you the best. The word that you think is most significant is called your *core belief* and it helps to mould, shape and create every aspect of your self-image; it underlies the way you see yourself.

My core belief is that I am:

. . . .

. . . .

Does this statement criticize you or appreciate you? Does it support high or low self-esteem? Don't despair if your core belief is deeply negative (it is for most of us). Once you know how you are sabotaging yourself you can begin to make radical, positive changes and this has got to be a good thing!

Step 5 Now write down your positive qualities.

My positive qualities are:

. . . .

. . . .

Even if your self-image is rather negative at the moment there are things that you *do* like about yourself. Give this some time, thought and consideration. A big hint here: focus on what you *can* do rather than what you *can't* do; think about your inner strengths, such as your determination to make changes and your belief that you can do this. What nice things would your best friend say about you?

Now, how do these great qualities of yours embellish your feelings of self-worth and self-esteem? And if you are still struggling to admire anything about wonderful you, then reflect on the inevitable consequences of this. The obstacles to your high self-esteem lie within. Why not choose to maximize your very best asset: your miraculous self!

Step 6 And finally, make a list of any characteristics that you think would further enhance your self-image. Really let yourself go here, be imaginative and aspirational. The more you can visualize these exciting new possibilities, the more likely they are to come true.

I would love to be:

. . . .

. . . .

How We are Programmed for Life

And by now you might be asking yourself just where all these beliefs have come from. As we begin to explore and discover the nature of some of the self-concepts that take away our self-esteem we naturally wonder why we ever bought into these lowering opinions in the first place. Why would that gorgeous openhearted, inquisitive and trusting baby, that was you, begin to believe that you were anything less than, well, gorgeous?

You arrived with a clean slate, with no judgemental, comparative or critical faculties; the doors were wide open to any possibility; the world was your oyster and you had nothing to prove. You were fascinated by life and in love with the world. If you take a look at some photos of yourself as a baby you will see your natural benevolence and intrinsic worth; you were truly fabulous, and you still are.

You learned how to feel about yourself and the world by imitating others during your formative years. As you developed you absorbed everything that you could; your eager and enquiring mind was just like a sponge mop sucking up anything and everything in its path. In our early years we can't rely on our own sense of judgment and reason, and so our unconscious mind busily accepts all the messages that are transmitted in our environment, whether they are happy, frightening, positive, negative, supportive, critical ... whatever. And so it is that we grow up being deeply affected by many of our parents' basic patterns of thinking, feeling and behaving. Because we internalized these messages, we took them for our own and so unconsciously programmed our minds to feel, think and behave in certain ways. Our personal development journey begins with this understanding: the nature of our experiences depends upon the nature of our patterns. In computer terminology this relationship between input and output is described as GIGO, 'garbage in, garbage out'. If our beliefs (what we have put *into* our mind) are negative and pessimistic then our output (how we experience our lives) will be the same. Happily, the opposite is true. When our beliefs are positive and optimistic then our thoughts, feelings and behaviour will be a reflection of them – creativity in, creativity out.

Once we fully understand the implications of our personal programming we have a most amazing tool for self-change: our beliefs are not set in stone, we can always change the programme.

INSIGHT

You can Magnetize Confidence

You are what you believe you are, and your expectations attract your experiences. This means that you can 'draw' positivity towards yourself by your thoughts, feelings and actions. Try getting into the skin of the confident you.

- Recollect the last time you were filled with exuberance and hope. If this is too hard just remember a happy occasion (go back as far as you need).

- Relive the scene, see the details in colour, feel your upbeat mood, step into your confident mode.

- Notice how much brighter you feel as you magnetize the power of positivity towards yourself once again.

- Repeat this process again and again until you can just create that positive vibration at will.

High self-esteem does not depend on worldly success and personal talents; it is an experience you can have whatever is going on in your life. When you next feel your mental energy sinking into your boots, start to magnetize a great new alternative mood for yourself. The more you do this the easier it gets. Increased self-esteem is only a thought away.

Consider this: *Your positive energy levels can be affected by the negative energy of others; some people can act like energy vampires.*

Case Study

Miranda, 35, works for a large international law firm which is based in the City. She has a fabulous job, which takes her all over the world and she meets a lot of interesting people, but when she spoke to me she said that she was feeling, '... washed out, burned out and unsure about myself, I have just lost all my enthusiasm and self-belief'. After years of buzzing around feeling pretty confident and good about herself, she had suddenly come to an emotional standstill. Miranda had been with her partner Richard for the last six years and they lived together in a flat that she owned. Richard had trained at RADA but had never really broken into the acting world and was always what he called 'between jobs', temping or waiting at tables and getting increasingly despondent. Miranda had been totally supportive of Richard from the start and as she said, '... kept him with a roof over his head and in the manner to which he was accustomed'. Miranda was reluctant to talk about their relationship and said that it was because she felt so guilty discussing him, and she agreed that she felt sorry for him. She said that she had always managed to stay one step ahead of his grumpiness and bad moods but was now finding it harder and harder to do so. Miranda admitted that she had never really been free to be herself with Richard because he was always having such a hard time, often becoming angry with her when she was successful at work or was sent on trips abroad. As she talked, it became more and more obvious that Miranda just couldn't maintain her positive, upbeat, supportive act when Richard was determined to 'drain' her energy. I think this is a useful word to use to describe what happens when one person effectively stonewalls the positive energy of another. Perhaps you have been in this situation yourself, when your help and encouragement only appears to fan the flames of even more negativity.

Miranda took a long time to finally move on from Richard and we spent many weeks talking about the guilt which kept her in the relationship. She often spoke about how 'lucky' she had been to fall on her feet and how hard it was for Richard to get a break; it appeared that Richard often complained that life had treated her much better than it had treated him. Eventually Miranda was able to see she was being victimized by Richard every time things went well for her, and this, combined with his financial dependence, finally led to the end of the relationship. In the end she had to walk away and sometimes this is the only way to maintain our confidence and self-respect in the face of relentless negativity.

It can be remarkably hard to recognize when our positive support is unappreciated or even unwelcome and in Day 4 we will be discussing this in more detail. For now, just notice the way others react to your optimism and confidence.

When your confidence is low you will be more inclined to let others treat you badly. As your self-worth rises you will find that other people will treat you with more respect.

Positive Thoughts are Bigger than Negative Thoughts

Al Koran was a famous magician/mentalist, author and inventor. Mentalism is the name given to a performing art in which its practitioners appear to demonstrate highly developed mental or intuitive abilities. Al made many appearances on the Ed Sullivan show and wrote a book in 1971 called *Bring Out the Magic in Your Mind*. I remember finding this book in the library and being blown away by it; I then bought it and read it many times and it is now completely dog-eared. Koran wrote that, 'When we send a thought out into this substance in which we all live, it sets up waves, and the positive thought is much bigger, giving a quicker tempo, a far greater vibration.' He used a good analogy to describe the power of positive belief. Imagine that you throw a pebble into a pond. The ripples then spread out in ever widening circles to reach the shore where they stop. Now if you throw in two stones, in different places at the same time, and they differ in weight and size, they will both set up ripples or waves which will converge on each other. At the point where the two sets meet there will be a struggle as one overwhelms the other and the waves of the larger stone will sweep over the ripples of the smaller one. The bigger (more positive) your thoughts the more powerfully and forcefully they will swamp the smaller (more negative) ones. Positive thoughts are like the biggest stone, they always have the biggest impact. Positive belief is the strongest magic of all.

EXERCISE

Visualize the Biggest Thought

(adapted from my book *Just Do It Now*)

Running alongside our thoughts we have the pictures of our thoughts. If your thoughts are self-validating then the pictures in your mind will reflect them and you will 'see' yourself achieving success and feeling happy. So a subtle way to change our thoughts is to change what we are imagining in our mind's eye. Rather than trying to delve around in our unconscious, attempting to discover negative images that hold us back, we can be proactive here and begin to visualize positive images instead.

You can use this brilliant visualization technique any time you find yourself suffering from negativity either about yourself, someone else, or the state of the world. Don't worry if you can't 'see' the images, 'knowing' they are there is just as effective. If you can relax and close your eyes then do so, but if you need a quick positive fix on the bus, in a meeting, in Tesco, or any place where there are others around then you can do it just as easily with your eyes open.

> The sun is shining in a beautiful clear blue sky and is being reflected in a small round pond. Perhaps there are bulrushes growing around the edge of the pond or bejewelled dragonflies swooping across its surface, maybe you can hear frogs croaking or birds singing nearby. Let your imagination take you where it will and create a vivid colourful picture complete with movement and sound. Absorb all the details and set the scene in your mind so that you can immediately recreate it at any time.
>
> See yourself standing at the edge of the pond, you are looking good and feeling confident. You bend down and pick up two

smooth brown pebbles; one is much bigger than the other. Hold one in each hand and feel the difference in weight between the two. Be aware of which hand holds which pebble. Now throw the pebbles into different parts of the pond. You watch as the circle of small ripples made by the lighter stone are overwhelmed by the circle of larger waves made by the heavier stone, and you know that, in just the same way, the positive thought you hold is big enough to overcome your smaller and limiting beliefs.

After you have done this visualization a number of times you can reach a stage where you see yourself throwing in only the larger pebble. This action symbolizes your desire to think only the biggest, highest and most positive thought. There is no need to worry about the exact nature of your biggest thought; it is enough to know that your intention is to go for the thought that creates the biggest wave.

I often use this visualization. Whenever I need an injection of positive energy, I just imagine throwing my large smooth pebble into the pond and know that I have chosen the highest thought (whatever that might turn out to be). Try this technique when you next need an energy boost, it only takes a few seconds. When you can hold the biggest thoughts about yourself and others, your days will become brighter and your confidence will grow.

Day 2 | Review

Key reflections for Day 2

- You can refuse to hold a negative belief.
- You will only begin to change when you can accept yourself as you are right now (human and therefore imperfect).
- By simply witnessing your negative thoughts (with no further judgment) you can loosen their hold over you and feel some kindness for yourself.
- If you are optimistic you will attract powerful positive energy, others will respond to your personal magnetism and your relationships will improve dramatically.
- Most of us have a negative core belief but we all have the power to change this situation. Once you know how you are self-sabotaging you can stop doing it.
- The obstacles to your high self-esteem lie within. You can decide to maximize your best asset: your miraculous self.
- By using positive visualization techniques you can quickly become the confident new you.
- You learned how to feel about yourself and the world by imitating others during your formative years.
- Once you understand the implications of your own personal programming you can break your habitual self-defeating patterns.
- High self-esteem does not depend on worldly success, it is an experience that you can have whatever is going on in your life.
- Some people are energy vampires who can drain you of your positive good intentions.
- The bigger, more positive thought will always overcome the smaller negative thought.

Your 3-Point Action Plan for Day 2

1 Take any insight that you have made today:
Example: *I let certain people drain me of positive energy and then I feel very low and unsure of myself.*

2 Consider the patterns (thought/emotional/behavioural) that might lie behind this:
Example: *I often feel guilty when others are feeling low; it's hard for me to keep positive and happy if someone else is struggling.*

3 Create an action point around a possible change of response:
Example: *I need to remember that: I can't change how anybody else feels; everyone is responsible for themselves; keeping positive is a kind and benevolent way to be.*

Try this 3-point action plan for yourself.

My personal insights:

. . . .

. . . .

The patterns that might lie behind this:

. . . .

. . . .

. . . .

My action points:

. . . .

. . . .

. . . .

Put your action points into practice and note your progress in your journal.

DAY 3

Feel Good

I want my boys to have an understanding of people's emotions, their insecurities, people's distress, and their hopes and dreams.

Diana, Princess of Wales

Day 3 | Feel Good

*If your emotional abilities aren't in hand, if you don't
have self-awareness, if you are not able to manage your
distressing emotions, if you can't have empathy and have
effective relationships, then no matter how smart you are,
you are not going to get very far.*

Daniel Goleman (psychologist)

When Daniel Goleman talks about our 'emotional abilities' he opens up an interesting new way for us to examine our feelings and gives us an empowering sense that we are not necessarily at the mercy of our emotions (although often it can feel as if we are). We know that the CBT model demonstrates the interrelationship between thought, feelings and actions, and that a change in any of these three will directly affect the other two. In Day 2 we began to look at the nature of our thoughts and how they ultimately affect our moods and our effectiveness in the world. Today we are considering the sensitive subject of our feelings and how we can develop and refine our emotional abilities so that we can be confident and balanced.

We can spend a lot of thought, time and money on making ourself as attractive as we can; pandering to the needs of the body we see in the mirror, and of course there is nothing wrong with this in moderation. But how do we care for our emotional bodies, what sort of attention do we pay our feelings?

Do you jump for joy when you are happy; feel miserable when your friend is sad; get upset when you watch distressing news footage; cry at weepy movies ...? Of course you do; these states are a natural expression of our being, our feelings are a part of us in just the same way as our physical bits and pieces are. But although we go to great lengths to keep up with the perceived needs of our physical body we are much less likely to give our emotional body anywhere near the same attention. And this is strange because if we don't look after our emotional needs properly we will be unhappy and very low in self-esteem. You might wonder how it's possible to take care of our emotions when they often appear to have a life of their own, taking us up and down again, alarmingly and unpredictably. Feelings come and go, they change in an instant. But when we can understand, respect and acknowledge why we feel the way we do, we immediately begin to take confident control of our lives.

How Do You Feel?

Would you describe yourself as an emotional or unemotional person?

Some people are acutely sensitive at the emotional level: they are very much in touch with their own feelings and also extremely aware of the feelings of others. If you are like this, you will certainly know it because this type of awareness can be difficult to handle. It is so easy to become swamped by emotion, whether it is our own or somebody else's. If we do become overwhelmed by feelings, our thoughts and actions will be immediately affected and our total experience will be limited. Think of a time when you got into a panic about something:

- What happened to you mentally?
- Did you experience any physical sensations?
- How did you behave?

When we feel at the mercy of our emotions we fall into a state of confusion; our judgment becomes clouded ('Is that the right thing to do?'); we may have physical symptoms (anxiety attacks, butterflies, tension headaches); our behaviour may not be what we expected it to be (perhaps we say yes when we wanted to say no, maybe we are too afraid to do what we had planned to do). It is difficult to react rationally when our emotions are in full flood.

On the other hand, there are those who appear to be acutely insensitive at the emotional level. Do you know anyone who is like this? These people seem to be quite unaffected by the emotional tides of life. The ability to operate rationally is a great gift but not if it is earned at the expense of our feelings. 'Supercool' may mean 'super-insensitive'. If we are not in touch with our own emotions we will remain unaware of the feelings of others. If we deny our feelings then we again limit our total experience. Think of a time when you strangled an emotion because you felt that it would be too painful for some reason:

- What happened to your thoughts?
- How did your body feel?
- How did you behave?

Super-rational or super-emotional, the price is high; it is the loss of a creative, validating and authentic experience and it will cost us our self-esteem. Our confidence and self-respect can only develop when we can balance our rationality and our emotions; we need both traits equally. Emotional awareness is a quality which helps us to cultivate the imaginative and creative parts of our nature and we shall see how very important it is to develop our sensitivity in these areas. However, in order to express our creativity we also need to be able to exercise our logical and rational abilities.

Super-rationality emerges when we deny our feelings and remain unaware of our imaginative and creative potential. This denial usually occurs because deep inside we are afraid of the power of our feelings. We are afraid that we will be overwhelmed and that we will lose control. It is curious, but true, that super-emotionality also develops from the denial of our feelings; we become oversensitive if we are suffering from a backlog of unexpressed emotions which we were afraid to express at the right time.

CONFIDENCE TIP

Love Your Feelings

- Stop for a moment and consider where you are coming from, right now in this present moment.

- Close your eyes and take stock of your emotional states.

- Just notice the ways that you are feeling without judging them, let them just be.

- Can you accept them just as they present themselves to you?

- Adopt an attitude of equanimity towards these feelings, neither trying to hang on to them nor trying to push them away.

- Stop striving; relax and let your uprising emotions just wash over you.

- Visualize these emotions as beautiful coloured bubbles that are drifting around your orbit and then drifting away again – and this is just what emotions do; they come and then go.

- Try a kind and compassionate approach to your emotional states, whatever they may be; this is the way to open your heart to yourself whatever you might be feeling.

- Stay with these feelings of acceptance and openheartedness and notice how this relaxed confident approach affects all your relationships today.

Your Deepest Feelings

We have seen that when we are high in self-esteem we experience certain feelings and that low self-esteem is associated with other feelings. When our self-esteem is low we may feel:

insecure	uptight	antisocial	depressed
victimized	guilty	worried	critical
stressed	afraid of our emotions		

EXERCISE

Discovering Your Core Emotions

Look at the list above and choose three emotional states that you have experienced when feeling low in self-esteem. Take one feeling at a time and write down any other feelings which you associate with it. Try to get right into the skin of the states you choose. Get right into the feeling and the *feeling behind the feeling* will emerge.

Example:

associated feelings:

Guilty
. . . .

anger with self

anger with others

resentment

fear of being found out

1 ....

associated feelings:

....

....

....

2 ....

associated feelings:

....

....

....

3 ....

associated feelings:

....

....

....

Are there any associated feelings which recur? If so what are they?

....

....

These recurring emotions are called *core emotions* and they are the deep feelings that lie *behind* what you might consider to be your more acceptable feelings. The example demonstrates that perhaps it is easier for me to admit that I feel guilty about something than it is for me to recognize my feelings of anger, fear and resentment. If anger, fear or resentment appeared again during this exercise then I would know that the repeating feeling was one of my core emotions. Our core emotions are usually feelings which we find difficult to acknowledge. Do you find your core emotions hard to accept?

But there are two pieces of good news: we all struggle with our 'unacceptable' feelings to some degree, so you are not alone here, and there is a creative solution to this difficulty. Post Impressionist painter, Paul Cézanne suggested that, 'Genius is the ability to renew one's emotions in daily experience.' In other words, our most innovative responses are freshly made *in the moment* and rely on our ability to acknowledge and express exactly what we feel, rather than falling back into old outworn reactive patterns. When we are high in self-esteem we respect our feelings and are able to communicate them appropriately. In this way we can ensure that we are not being ruled by our emotions. When we can accept all our feelings we will no longer be trapped in behaviour which is either extremely rational or extremely emotional. A healthy and balanced emotional life requires that we take the following three steps:

Step 1   experience a feeling

Step 2   recognize and accept this feeling

Step 3   express and let go of this feeling

If we don't go through this process we will experience a build-up of denied and unexpressed emotion. If we suppress our feelings for long enough the chances are that we will become so out of touch with our emotional state that we won't even know what our feelings are any more; new feelings will be lost in our emotional confusion and so the build-up of unexpressed emotion continues. There have been so many times when I have asked clients what they feel about something that has affected them greatly and they have answered that they don't know. The coaching process then involves the unravelling of a tangled ball of feelings in order to clarify the nature of the individual emotional strands.

Can you think of a time when a minor incident occurred and you completely overreacted? Perhaps something quite sad happened and you felt overwhelmed by grief. Maybe a small irritating episode sent you into a great storm of anger. Whenever we deny our feelings, we can't release them. We can never let go of anything until we first acknowledge its existence. So denial leads to holding on, which means that these feelings that we cannot accept become hidden away inside us. These secret feelings may be buried so deeply that we do not even recognize their existence any more. Our secret feelings (hidden from others and maybe even hidden from ourselves) can create imbalance at all levels of our being: mind, body, spirit and emotions. Suppressed emotions lie within us just waiting to attract our attention in some way: they may erupt at an inappropriate time; reveal themselves in dreams or even cause us to be ill. One thing is for sure; their existence will always guarantee that we stay low in self-esteem.

We cannot respect ourselves if we are denying our true feelings. Our feelings are directly associated with our needs. If we are feeling good our needs are being met and if we don't feel good it is because our needs are not being fulfilled. Whenever we deny our feelings we are actually denying our needs; we are telling ourselves, and the world, that our needs don't count and so our self-esteem will be at an all-time low! So here we find a key that opens the door to a new, confident and assertive you. If you are low in self-esteem at the moment, you could ask yourself if your needs are being met, and if not, why not? There will be some unravelling and clarifying to be done but this can easily be accomplished. But before we look at this process let's lift our energy by infusing ourselves with some positive emotions.

Your Positive Emotional Qualities

Whatever you focus your attention on will grow: if you keep looking at your difficult issues then that is all you will see. And although you need to look to the roots of your limiting patterns so that you can identify, accept and release them, it is important to balance this with a recognition of your wonderful, natural and positive energy.

10 ways to feel fabulous

1 *Give optimism a chance.* If you are more of an Eeyore than a Tigger then just give this a try. Suspend all pessimistic thoughts and be optimistic for one day. Notice how this affects you.

2 *Enjoy the success of others.* Sharing the good feelings of other people is a surprisingly easy way to open your heart.

3 *Remember your kindness.* Think of the last time you were kind to someone (even very small acts of kindness count).

4 *Be an encourager.* What can you do to support yourself and someone else today?

5 *Visualize a positive outcome.* Expect the best and 'see' it happening, what does this action do to your spirits?

6 *Focus on your best qualities.* Look at your strong inner resources here. What a survivor you are!

7 *Contact someone you love.* Make that important connection and feel your heart respond.

8 *Try a spot of cloudgazing.* In other words, stop, slow down and enjoy this wonderful moment.

9 *Notice goodwill* wherever you see it today: on a train, walking down the road, in a supermarket, on the road ... How does the kindness of others affect you?

10 *Develop your inner smile.* This is your response to any appreciative, contented moment – cultivate these feelings.

Going into Denial and Coming out Again

As we grew out of babyhood we began to curtail the natural self-expression of our emotions because most of us learned, at a very early age, that our feelings were best kept to ourselves. The root cause of this emotional denial lies in fear, and we learned about this fear from our parents and others who influenced our perceptions in our early years. Feelings are powerful energy, and in the adult world there is a widespread fear that emotional expression might lead to loss of control. And because our feelings are an expression of our needs, there is another fear: if we show that we are 'needy' in any way, we will be revealing our weaknesses and so will become vulnerable.

Our culture is full of familiar messages which encourage children to keep a stiff upper lip. Did you hear any of these when you were young?*'Don't be afraid ... Boys don't cry ... When you get angry I can't take it ... You shouldn't feel like that ... Don't cry, it's babyish ... Just grin and bear it ... Jealousy is so unattractive ... When you get miserable I feel terrible ... Just pretend you don't care ... Don't talk about death it is too upsetting ... If you say what you think people won't like you ... Little girls should always look pretty ...'* What can you add to this list?

These ideas may have been spoken messages or they might have been passed on in a more subtle way. We learn our beliefs about the way this world works in many different ways. Children often internalize messages which are not actually spoken out loud; the subtler messages of our childhood can nevertheless have profound effects in our adulthood. We have learned and absorbed so much from the vibrations which surrounded our early upbringing. Thought, feeling and behaviour patterns permeate our lives and we experience them at every level; physical, mental, emotional and spiritual. We learn as much from what is left unsaid as from what is said. The raised eyebrow; the smile that never quite reached the eyes; a spoken acceptance with body language demonstrating rejection; the cold feeling which comes from being ignored. There are so many ways that we can learn from unspoken messages.

EXERCISE

Remembering Unspoken Messages

What did you learn from the unspoken messages of your childhood? You might have to think very deeply before you can complete this exercise; the messages may have been quite subtle but the implications will be profound.

Example:

1 The unspoken message was:
  My father ignored me whenever I disagreed with him.

2 What I learned from this was:
  If I always pretended to agree with my father he would give me attention.

3 The implications of this are:
  I am now often unable to speak my mind and this makes me very angry.

1 The unspoken message was:

....

....

....

....

2 What I learned from this was:

....

....

....

....

3 The implications of this are:

....

....

....

....

Let Your Star Shine Brightly

We usually talk about denial in terms of our not wanting to look at 'bad' stuff, so we repress it and it becomes shadow material. But there is another take on this which is wonderfully liberating and removes the 'dark' feeling that can surround the idea of our shadow (denied, repressed parts of self). As we are so adept at denial it is entirely likely that we are actually repressing some of our natural creative responses which for some reason we have learned to mistrust. Take a look at the list below:

- Kind

- Clever

- Generous

- Trusting

- Talented

- Loving

- Thoughtful

- Responsive

Now give yourself a score from 1 to 10 for each of these qualities, 1 being the lowest and 10 the highest score. If you scored below 5 for anything on this list just consider if your evaluation is actually true. Could it be that you are under-estimating yourself? Are you hiding away from reaching your potential? Are you denying your stellar qualities?

Try adopting an open-minded and openhearted approach to all that you are. Imagine you are ready to accept that you have all the positive qualities on this list and more! You score 10 for every one. Suspend all disbelief for the moment and appreciate your sheer wonderfulness. How does this feel? Perhaps your first assessment was based on a pattern of low self-worth. Try overriding this today and demonstrate to yourself how kind, clever, generous, trusting, talented, loving, thoughtful and responsive you can be. Be a bright star for others.

It's time to drop those negative thoughts about yourself, they are only getting in your way. Never mind whatever it is that you think you can't do – concentrate instead on what you can do.

EXERCISE

Accepting and Expressing Emotions

We all find some feelings harder to accept and to express than others. Fill in the Table of Emotions, with a tick in the relevant column for each feeling, to see what you find easy and what you find hard. Again, you may find the need to think very carefully before doing this exercise. Really think your answers through.

Table of Emotions

	ACCEPTING			EXPRESSING		
	easy	sometimes difficult	always difficult	easy	sometimes difficult	always difficult
FEELING						
sadness						
shame						
happiness						
anger						
delight						
grief						
dislike						
friendliness						
fear						
jealousy						

	ACCEPTING			EXPRESSING		
	easy	sometimes difficult	always difficult	easy	sometimes difficult	always difficult
worry						
love						
vulnerability						
frustration						
caring						
aloneness						
rejection						
depression						
enthusiasm						

What did the Table of Emotions show you? Were you surprised by any of your answers? Look at the feelings that are always difficult to accept. Consider why you find these emotions so hard to deal with.

Maybe you learned as a child that these particular feelings were taboo in some ways. For example, if you showed your love and then felt rejected, it might be too terrifying for you to show your loving feelings now. Perhaps you grew up in a very angry environment, where people were never able to release their anger at the appropriate time and so were always operating on the edge of a volcano of feelings. Some people are angry all their lives and they never discover the root of their anger; they might react to this by discharging anger continually or they may show absolutely no emotion. Extremely hurt and angry people may eventually be numbed by the intensity of their own feelings. If we are really hurting we can try to defend ourselves by moving into a non-feeling mode. So, angry people might come in disguise and, although they don't raise their voice, the air can be filled with their numbed rage. Think about who was angry in your house and how they showed (or didn't show) that anger.

Did you find some feelings easy to accept but difficult to express? Although acceptance must come before the expression of a feeling, it doesn't follow that if you can easily accept a feeling you will necessarily find it easy to express it. Acceptance is one part of the letting-go process and it is the first step, but sharing your feelings is something else. For example, perhaps I can accept my own grief but find it very difficult to express this feeling to anyone else, worrying about what they will think, or whether they can handle it. 'Can they handle it?' is a big consideration.

Many people are very afraid of their emotions for all the reasons which we have looked at. These folk 'can't handle it'. They send unspoken messages that say:

1 Don't show me your emotions,

because ...   2 I am afraid of your emotions,

because ...   3 I am afraid of my own emotions

and so ...   4 I want you to keep your feelings to yourself.

When you are ready to share an emotion find someone who *can* handle it. Those who have done some work on releasing their own feelings find it easier to be a listening ear for others. At some point you might feel the need for help: professional coaching/counselling or joining a support group. But you can also work on yourself very effectively.

Consider this: *The emotions that you are most afraid to feel can have an amazingly transformative effect on your life.*

Case Study

Kathy, 42, was a primary school teacher who had just been offered a much wanted deputy headship at another school. She contacted me because she was experiencing what she called a 'huge confidence crisis' since being offered the post. Kathy said that she had sailed through the application and interview process and, in theory, should have been over the moon. I asked her when her feelings started to become uncomfortable and she said it all began when she had an informal chat with her new head (who we shall call Emma), just after she accepted the post.

Recounting the experience Kathy said, 'I breezed into that appointment full of excitement and confidence and came out with my self-esteem in tatters. Emma was lovely, almost too lovely and there was just something about her that felt quite threatening to me. She did everything to make me feel at my ease but the friendlier she was the more guarded and stilted I became. I just about got through the meeting and then rushed back home and burst into tears; suddenly I didn't want my great new job, everything felt too overwhelming and I was considering turning down the offer. I tried to talk about it with my partner but he just said I was being totally illogical and I needed to get a grip. Things got worse and I was unable to go in to teach my class.

'Then my twin sister Mel dropped by, en route to some glitzy publishing meeting, and asked me what was going on and I felt absolutely incandescent with rage. I told her it was none of her business and I was quite rude to her and she left quickly. Our relationship history is patchy and very up and down. I am always on edge when she is around and feel like I have been running to catch up with her since we were born – she is 20 minutes older than me. Mel was prettier, cleverer and more talented than me in every respect and definitely dad's favourite girl. Actually after Mel left I realized that she reminded me of Emma and that in the meeting at the new school I had begun to compare myself unfavourably with Emma (who is tall and blonde like Mel).'

As we talked more about her childhood Kathy realized, much to her great shame, that she had always been jealous of her twin's successes and still was. Once she had admitted this to me, Kathy felt a lot better and was able to go back to work. We then spent a few sessions considering if she could change the way she felt about Mel and if it was possible to let go of the jealousy that was having such a stranglehold on her.

Kathy used a strategy called 'witnessing' which is a way of stepping out of a reactive emotional place to achieve a clearer, calmer and more objective state. You can do this too, by just deciding to adopt the role of 'onlooker'. In this way you can become less attached to your powerful emotions and have a more relaxed response.

Kathy had a strong intention to change and it was this that helped her more than anything. She was ready to accept her difficult feelings and to begin to let them go. As she was able to reach out to her twin their relationship began to blossom and they got to know each other in a totally new way, which was such a great confidence boost to both of them. Kathy took the job of course and began a friendship with Emma. And the moral of this story is that: although our troublesome unexpressed feelings can become very complex and tangled, it is always possible to unravel them and, in doing so, to open up a brand new chapter in our lives.

EXERCISE

Letting Go of Emotions

You can use this process at any time when you are troubled by your feelings. It will help to clarify your true emotions.

Take an emotion that you find difficult to accept and to express.
    Write,
'I (name) am denying that I feel (emotion).'

For example, I might write:
    I, Lynda, am denying that I feel ashamed.

1   *I* . . . .

      am denying that I feel . . . .

Get a large sheet of paper, a pen, a mirror and a large box of tissues. Now write this statement over and over. Once you have finished writing it then say it over and over. Notice all the feelings that are coming up for you. When you are ready, look into your own eyes in the mirror and repeat this statement. If this is hard just *stick at it*: mirror work is a very profound experience. If you are feeling very emotional then express it in some way. You may have a bucketful of tears inside you; you might want to bash the stuffing out of a pillow; you may just want to curl up under the duvet and go to sleep. Do whatever feels right. You might feel unmoved and that's fine too, it doesn't matter if nothing seems to be happening to you.

Continue the letting-go process no matter how you are feeling.
Repeat the same process for all parts of this exercise.

2 I
. . . .

am denying that I feel
. . . .

because
. . . .

If you can use the mirror then do so; this speeds up the process
no end. What is it like to look yourself in the eyes in this way?

3 I
. . . .

am ready to accept that I feel
. . . .

4 I
. . . .

accept that I feel
. . . .

5 I
. . . .
love and value all my experiences.

6 I
. . . .
love and value all my feelings.

7 I
. . . .

give myself permission to feel
. . . .

You are now allowing yourself to *fully experience* the denied feelings. If you are experiencing other feelings then just acknowledge them. You may feel guilty or angry with yourself. If you do, then complete the following.

8 I .... *forgive myself.*

Do you feel angry with anyone else? If so, forgive them.

9 I ....

forgive you ....

And so you can express your feelings in many different ways. We have been inhibited about connecting with our most powerful emotions because deep down we imagine that these emotions can *cause* us pain. But actually this is not true. It is *resistance* to feeling that causes our pain. If you are afraid of a feeling and suppress it, you will feel pain. If you go with the feeling, then your experience might be very intense but it will not hurt you. Your feelings cannot harm you; they have no power over you; they are an integral part of your self-expression. Remember that *you create* your own feelings and that they are a colourful demonstration of your unique individuality.

When you can love and value yourself, whatever you may be feeling, you will no longer be at the mercy of your emotions; you will be respecting all your feelings and will be able to express them appropriately. And when your emotional life is balanced you will be high in self-esteem.

Day 3 | Review

Key Reflections for Day 3

- You are not at the mercy of your feelings; you can develop and refine your emotional abilities so that you can feel confident and balanced.
- It is very difficult to react rationally when our emotions are in full flood.
- Feelings come and go, they change in an instant, but as soon as you can understand, respect and acknowledge why you feel the way you do, you immediately begin to take confident control of your life.
- Your confidence and self-respect will only develop when you can balance your rationality and your emotions; you need both traits equally.

- We cannot respect ourselves if we are denying our true feelings.
- Try adopting a kind and compassionate approach to your emotional states, whatever they may be; this is the way to open your heart to yourself whatever you may be feeling.
- Whatever you concentrate your attention upon will grow, so it is wise to focus on your positive emotional qualities.
- Develop your inner smile; this is your natural heartfelt response to any peaceful and appreciative moment.
- Most people are very afraid of their emotions.
- Your feelings cannot harm you; they have no power over you because you have created them yourself.
- Imagine that you are ready to accept that you are full of positive qualities and notice how this make you feel.

Your 3-Point Action Plan for Day 3

1 Take any insight that you have made today:
Example: *I realized that I am afraid of showing my anger.*

2 Consider the patterns (thought/emotional/behavioural) that might lie behind this:
Example: *My mother always suppressed her anger to keep the peace and I do exactly the same.*

3 Create an action point around a possible change of response:
Example: *I have decided to start acknowledging when I am angry and then to look at the reasons for these feelings rather than just dismissing them as unimportant or too frightening.*

Try this 3-point action plan for yourself.

My personal insights:

....

....

....

The patterns that might lie behind this:

....

....

....

My action points:

....

....

....

Day 4

Act Assertively

If you deliberately plan to be less than you are capable of being, then I want to warn you that you'll be deeply unhappy the rest of your life.

Abraham Maslow (psychologist)

Day 4 | Act Assertively

*I wish I'd known from the beginning that I was born a
strong woman. What a difference it would have made! I
wish I'd known that I was born a courageous woman; I've
spent so much of my life cowering. How many conversa-
tions would I not only have started but **finished** if I had
known I possessed a warrior's heart? I wish I'd known
that I'd been born to take on the world; I wouldn't have
run from it for so long, but **to** it with open arms.*

Sarah Ban Breathnach (author)

I love the images provoked by this piece. A 'strong woman'; what
do you see when you read that? And 'cowering'; yes you will know
what that sort of behaviour looks and feels like; we have all played
the victim at one time or another. A warrior's heart has been yours all
along but maybe you have forgotten this; if so, remember it now. How
does it feel to stand in your beautiful, shiny, courageous shoes? When
we can open our arms to the world, and in particular to the miracle
of our own existence, we can believe in ourselves, feel confident and
act assertively. Day 4 is all about embracing the dynamic, proactive
and determined you. When you are being authentic (real and true to
yourself) then your behaviour will be naturally assertive and you will
act like a winner. Being assertive does not come naturally to many of
us; but it is a skill that we can all develop, and today we are going to
investigate exactly how we can do this.

It's Not What You do but the Way that You do it

On Day 3 we saw how important it is to stay in touch with our true feelings so that we can ask for and get what we need to make us happy. Today we are going to look at different models of behaviour to see which is most effective in bringing us closer to our goals, and so increasing our feelings of self-worth. We will be considering the answers to the following questions:

- What does it mean to act like a winner?
- What type of behaviour creates high self-esteem?
- Why do we sometimes behave like a victim?
- How can we raise our game and act assertively?

We teach people how to treat us. What is your first reaction to this statement? Do you believe it or not? Much more important than *what* we do is *how* we do it. If we are looking for a successful outcome from our actions then we need to understand how the different behavioural styles create different results. It is simply a question of recognizing the inevitable relationship between cause and effect. If we act like a victim then others will treat us like one, and if we respond creatively and courageously then others will treat us with the respect we deserve.

There will always be a direct link between the way that you behave and your level of self-esteem. Whenever you make an assertive response you are acting like one of life's winners. In this context a winner is defined as someone who always makes the most of their potential, does the very best they can whatever the circumstances, and maintains a positive approach even in the face of extreme adversity. A winner makes non-victim responses and knows the magic formula that creates a winning situation:

| self-belief | + | positive emotions | + | assertive action | = | winning outcome |

Figure 5 shows the range of options that are open to us in any social interaction. If we act assertively then we are respecting our needs, as well as the needs of others, and so of course we will feel confident and sure of ourselves. In order to respond assertively we need to: know what we want (and what we don't want); be ready to take total responsibility for the life we have created; have open and honest communication with others and be prepared to take a chance.

'Victim' behaviour can be *aggressive* or *passive* or anywhere in between. If we are acting the victim then we are angry and resentful; we blame people for the things that happen to us; we have poor communication skills; we are afraid to show our true feelings and we are insecure and have no self-respect. If our self-esteem is low we feel like losers and can only operate in this victim mode.

How the Passive-Aggressive-Passive Cycle Operates

If we act like a victim we can find ourselves swinging between the extremes of the aggressive and passive styles. This is how it works.

- Imagine that something happens and I feel psychologically threatened.
- I withdraw immediately into the *passive* mode, become defensive and feel sorry for myself.
- I hold on to my feelings of resentment (and let them stew).
- Then at some point, and usually at a totally inappropriate time, I burst forth in an *aggressive* attack.
- Then, consumed by guilt and remorse, I swing back into the *passive* mode.

Do you recognize this cycle? Of course not everyone swings between these two extremes. Some people specialize in the passive style while others use aggressive tactics. At first it might seem that these two modes are completely different: an aggressor is loud and domineering and might seem determined and confident, in contrast to the passive

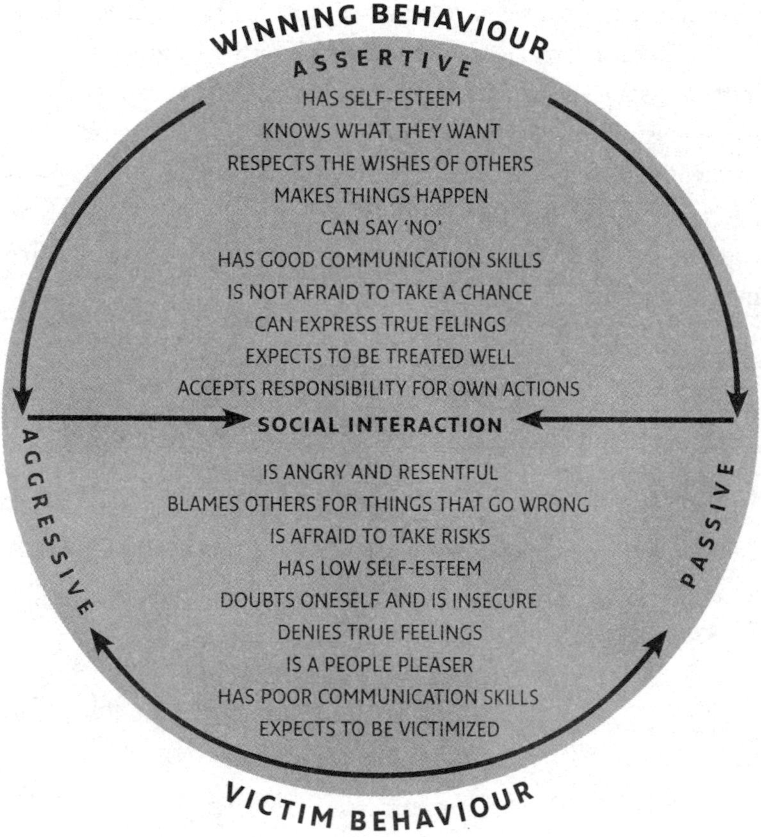

WINNING BEHAVIOUR

ASSERTIVE

HAS SELF-ESTEEM

KNOWS WHAT THEY WANT

RESPECTS THE WISHES OF OTHERS

MAKES THINGS HAPPEN

CAN SAY 'NO'

HAS GOOD COMMUNICATION SKILLS

IS NOT AFRAID TO TAKE A CHANCE

CAN EXPRESS TRUE FELINGS

EXPECTS TO BE TREATED WELL

ACCEPTS RESPONSIBILITY FOR OWN ACTIONS

SOCIAL INTERACTION

Aggressive

Passive

IS ANGRY AND RESENTFUL

BLAMES OTHERS FOR THINGS THAT GO WRONG

IS AFRAID TO TAKE RISKS

HAS LOW SELF-ESTEEM

DOUBTS ONESELF AND IS INSECURE

DENIES TRUE FEELINGS

IS A PEOPLE PLEASER

HAS POOR COMMUNICATION SKILLS

EXPECTS TO BE VICTIMIZED

VICTIM BEHAVIOUR

Figure 5: Two Different Models of Behaviour

person who has a quiet approach and appears to lack confidence and direction. But actually both styles are manipulative and blaming, and they are both ineffective.

I am sure that you recognize these victim and non-victim behaviour patterns; we have all acted in these three modes at one time or another. If we are feeling low in self-worth we are bound to find ourselves somewhere in the victim category; whether acting passively or aggressively – when our self-esteem is low we can only act like a victim. Conversely, when we are feeling good about ourselves, upbeat and confident we can act assertively and 'make things happen'; we can only operate in the winning (non-victim) mode when we are high in self-esteem.

EXERCISE

Types of Behaviour

Can you think of a time when you behaved in each of the three ways?

1 A time when I behaved passively

The situation was:

. . . .

The way I behaved was:

. . . .

The outcome of the situation was:

. . . .

2 A time when I behaved aggressively

The situation was:

....

The way I behaved was:

....

The outcome of the situation was:

....

....

3 A time when I behaved assertively

The situation was:

....

The way I behaved was:

....

The outcome of the situation was:

....

....

CONFIDENCE TIP

You Can if You Think You Can

- List your past achievements and go back as far as you like: *learning to ride a bike, passing an exam, getting a job, your first love affair....* Write these things down on a big sheet of paper and keep adding to the list. You have had so many successes.

- Remember that big challenge that you overcame, how did you cope? What inner resources do you fall back on? Name these and know that you have these qualities in abundance.

- Think back to a time when you were afraid to do something but did it anyway. Each time we leave our comfort zone we refresh and invigorate our energy. You know how to take a chance and you can do this again.

- You have all it takes to do what you want to do in this life; all you have to do is take that very first step. Take it today!

Going From Victim to Winner

My interest in personal development really took off once I realized that to a large degree I was creating my own reality. This understanding completely blew my cover: I couldn't carry on blaming anybody any more: parents, ex-husband, boss, traffic wardens, builders ... etc. (in extremis I even used to blame the weather). Once realization set in it didn't take long to get to grips with the fact that each and every time it was *someone else's fault* I gave away my own power to change things. If my father was really to blame for my low self-esteem then this meant I had no hope of becoming confident unless he changed in some way.

Similarly, if my ex-husband was responsible for my inability to trust men then I had absolutely no chance of ever having another relationship. I only came to terms with my addiction to playing the victim when my first marriage ended and I was living with my two toddlers (then aged 3 and 1).

The choice was stark: to keep complaining and blaming (indulging in victim consciousness) or to change my whole approach and get a life. I have to say that I didn't change overnight; it took some real effort as there were many negative patterns that I was wedded to. But as I read and understood more about the power of positive thinking, emotional intelligence and assertive action, I became hooked on self-help instead! And of course this passion of mine developed into a lifelong interest and a fabulous career – who would have guessed it? So, if you are indulging in any victim-like behaviour and don't want to do this any more, I can promise you that you can change; because if I can do it then so can you.

Of course there are reasons why you fall into the state of mind called victim consciousness. At first glance it might seem attractive to hand over the responsibility for your happiness to someone else; you can blame 'them' and remain unaccountable for whatever happens in your life. But why would you want to do this? Why is this sometimes such an appealing option? There are a number of possible explanations for this. It might be because you feel afraid to stand up for yourself or that you want people to like you, or that you are just too low to take any initiative. Don't be too hard on yourself here; we all know what it is like to behave like a victim. When we are severely challenged we are all inclined to become defensive and blaming, it is a natural response. Here we are just acknowledging the two types of behaviour in order that you can check out your present status and discover how to step out of victim mode and into winning mode.

How would you describe yourself right now? Are you 'making things happen' (proactive) or do you feel like 'things are just happening' to you (reactive)? If you are being proactive then you are assertive, confident, resourceful and high in self-esteem. And if you are being reactive then you have given away your power to other people; you are a victim of the actions of others and will be low in self-esteem. But remember, you can change this behaviour!

How Assertive are You?

Check out your behaviour status by answering the following questions.

At home
1 Does your family ever take you for granted?
2 Do you do more than your share of the domestic work?
3 Would you like more time just for yourself?
4 Is it hard to say 'no' to family members?
5 Do you ever buy clothes and hide them from your partner?

At work
6 Does your job interest you?
7 Are your colleagues appreciative and supportive?
8 Do you always work late when asked, even if you don't want to?
9 Are you able to express your opinions if you disagree with your boss?
10 Would you like to work somewhere else?

Being yourself
11 Do you often compare yourself with others?
12 You have achieved a success and someone compliments you. Are you able to accept this gracefully or do you brush it off?

13 Do you often feel intimidated when you meet new people?

14 Would you like to be more relaxed with others?

15 Do you ever find yourself apologizing for your behaviour?

In a relationship

16 Does your partner make you feel good about yourself?

17 If 'yes' how do they do this? If 'no' how do they do this?

18 Do you have any shared goals?

19 Are you waiting for your partner to change?

20 Do you still fancy your partner? If 'no' why are you together?

Out in the world

21 You reserve a table at a restaurant and find it is at the back near the door to the kitchen? Do you ask to be moved?

22 A pair of shoes split a month after you bought them, would you take them back? Would you feel anxious if you did?

23 You think that your child is being bullied at school, would you investigate further? Would you ever make a complaint?

24 You are on a diet and friends try to persuade you to eat fish and chips with them. What do you do?

25 Your partner is over the limit but insists on driving. Do you allow it, call a taxi or insist that you drive?

Consider the implications of your answers. Notice the situations where you find it easy to stand up for yourself and those where you don't. Where are you most susceptible to letting others walk all over you?

The Doormat Syndrome

Most of us allow ourselves to be victimized sometimes; we all have our own particular areas of vulnerability. It might be easy for you to assert yourself at work but not at home with your children or in your intimate relationships. Sometimes I suggest to clients that rather than taking off their 'work hat' as soon as they step over their own threshold, they might try keeping it on for a while and employing some assertiveness techniques with their nearest and dearest. Women frequently say to me that the mixed feelings of guilt, resentment and love that they feel for their families often make it harder to enforce clear boundaries. And of course as soon as we operate with unclear boundaries we begin losing our self-respect and confidence. People with high self-esteem maintain boundaries that are safe for them whilst also remaining flexible enough to change if the need arises. We will be looking in greater detail at this important notion of clear and safe boundaries on Day 9 (*Have Brilliant Relationships*). Perhaps you feel confident in the areas of your life which are familiar, but find yourself intimidated when faced with a new situation.

It can be difficult to know whether we are being victimized or whether we are just operating from the goodness of our heart. If a friend asks for your help and you have another commitment, what do you do? If you help and cancel your own plans, are you acting like a victim or are you being a good friend? It isn't always easy to decide whether your needs come before or after the needs of someone else; there is often a very fine line between being genuinely helpful and being a victim of another person's needs. But there is a way to make a clear distinction.

EXERCISE

Are You Acting Like a Victim?

Think of a situation where you are unsure whether you are acting like a victim or not.

1 The situation is:

. . . .

2 How I behave:

. . . .

3 My feelings at the time are of :

. . . .

4 My thoughts at the time are:

. . . .

Whenever you are in doubt about the nature of your actions, look to the feelings and thoughts that you are experiencing.

Clues to victim status are to be found in *feelings* such as:

> Fear
> Intimidation
> Anger
> Resentment
> Irritation
> Helplessness
> Low self-esteem

Vulnerability
Exasperation

Clues to victim status are to be found in such underlying *thoughts* as:
I'm not as good as ...
I want you to like me
I can't say no
You are more deserving than me
I can't express my feelings
I am afraid of you
You always get your own way
I don't value my opinion
Nobody thinks much of me

Look back at your answers to the exercise. Are any of your thoughts and feelings about your particular situation included in these lists or did you come up with something else?

The meaning of our actions always lies in our intention. What are your true motives? What do you really feel? Deep down you will always know the answers to these questions. It can be very challenging to face the fact that you are doing something you don't really want to do. Sometimes we build our lives around the needs of others and once we start to recognize this we may unleash a volcano of anger which can feel very frightening. However, we don't have to react in an outrageous fashion: we can change our situation by teaching our victimizers some new ways to behave around us.

Becoming Assertive

A non-victim response is an assertive response. You are assertive when you act in your own best interests and stand up for yourself. You communicate your needs clearly and you also respect the rights and feelings of other people. You value yourself and others and you are high in self-esteem.

We teach other people the way we want them to treat us by being open and honest about what we really want/don't want to do. How can you know my true feelings about something unless I tell you? Unfortunately, a certain level of communication breakdown can often occur in long-standing relationships where one person thinks that they can predict the innermost thoughts and feelings of another. We can create a victimizing situation (which is of course characterized by its no-win nature) by expecting another person to know what we are thinking: 'I shouldn't have to *tell* you what I am thinking/feeling/ wanting, you should just *know.' Never* expect anyone to know your needs and desires; if you do, you will always feel let down, you will always feel like a victim. Just tell people clearly what you want; communicate your needs, it makes life so much simpler.

I have an acquaintance, who is well known as a 'good sort' because she will do anything for anybody at any time. Whatever I ask her to do for me; I know that she will say yes. She says yes to everyone and her house is often full of other people's children and she never has any time for herself. She will *always* put others' needs before her own and she has very little sense of her own worth. If we are denying our own needs then we have to address this so that we can raise our self-esteem.

Another friend, who is not known as a 'good sort' but is well respected, has a totally different approach. If I ask her a favour and she can't help me, she will always say so. As she is able to say no, I feel much happier asking her because I know where I stand with her. When you know you are 'using' a victim it leaves an uncomfortable feeling.

INSIGHT

You Can Decide To Take Control

When enough is enough, it is time to take a stand; on behalf of your wellbeing, happiness and self-esteem. Try some of these ways to get yourself moving in the right direction.

- *Give yourself a good start.* Begin your day calmly. Be aware that today you are starting to change your attitude and your behaviour. Remind yourself that you are taking control of your life again; doesn't that feel good?

- *Take a risk.* Confidence is a quality we develop *after* we have done the scary thing we think we can't do because we haven't got the confidence!

- *Be content with your best.* Perfectionist tendencies will keep you trapped in a negative spiral of low self-esteem.

- *Consider the alternative.* A confident and happy life, or the life of a loser? There simply is no choice is there?

- *Do something positive to activate a goal.* It doesn't matter how small a step you take because it will lead on to the next step and the next and the next...

Becoming a non-victim also requires that we become non-victimizers.

Remember that, in this context, we are using the notion of 'victim behaviour' to mean the way we act when we give our power away in any situation and let another person become our 'victimizer'. In this sense we are 'allowing' another person to bully us; we are 'inviting' their domineering behaviour. When we put an end to this we do ourselves and them a great favour!

- *Stop thinking badly about yourself.* Notice any negative thought patterns today and mentally blow them away as if they were fluffy clouds in a beautiful blue sky.

- *Say what you mean.* Why would you ever say something that you didn't mean?

- *Be optimistic.* By behaving in a positive and upbeat fashion you will *contradict* any negative patterns. Just for today give everyone and everything the BOD (benefit of the doubt). Notice how nice this feels.

- *Don't give up on yourself.* Be your own best supporter and fan! When you believe in yourself you can easily follow through.

- *Love your life.* As soon as you do this your life will start to love you back; try this now.

- *Keep it light.* Stay in touch with your sense of humour and don't confuse self-awareness with endless navel-gazing.

Consider this: *A firm decision to step into your confident shoes is all it takes to regain control of your life.*

Case Study

Clare, 29, is a web designer who runs her own company and she is confident, outgoing, and enjoys a great social life. I met her through a mutual friend and when she heard I was writing this book she told me a story about her early days as a student. Clare came from a large working-class family in Liverpool and her parents encouraged her to do well at school so that she could, as her mother put it: 'Get on in life and not end up on the dole like a lot of the kids round here.'

After winning a scholarship to a local independent school, Clare became an outstanding student and eventually went to Cambridge to study history. Clare said, 'When I got accepted at Cambridge I was really over the moon and full of confidence in my abilities; I couldn't wait to leave Liverpool and get on with my smart new life. But from the start I was so miserable. Back home I had been a bit of a celebrity on our estate and on the day I left for Cambridge loads of people came to see me off. In contrast, when I arrived in Cambridge I felt totally insignificant, and even worse I felt stupid, outclassed and out of my league. All the other girls seemed to have such privileged backgrounds and they all had such posh accents, I was afraid to even open my mouth.

'That first term was really bad and I only managed to make a couple of friends and they were shy bookworms. I was desperate when I went home that first Christmas and I didn't want to go back. I broke down and told mum what it was like and how miserable I was, and she was brilliant. She reminded me how hard I had worked to get there and how I deserved my place. I was really low in confidence by then and she said I just had to get a grip and go back firing on all cylinders.

'I had a new stylish haircut and decided to brazen it out; acting confidently even if I didn't feel it. I joined the drama club as soon as I got back and that's where things started to turn around. I made friends and regained my buzz, and suddenly the world was a wonderful place again. Whenever I have a confidence crisis nowadays I think back to that time and how low I got, and how a decision to make a go of it really transformed me. I would tell anyone who is feeling low in self-esteem that they have the power to change their feelings and behave differently – a firm decision to change will start that positive ball rolling.'

EXERCISE

Raising Your Game and Acting Like a Winner

Think of a situation where you know you are being victimized.

1   The situation is:

. . . .

Describe the ways that you behave when you are being over-accommodating.

2   I act like a victim by:

. . . .

And how are you feeling when you behave in this way?

3   I feel:

. . . .

What sort of thoughts are you having when you are being victimized?

4   I am thinking that:

. . . .

What messages are you conveying to your victimizer about your thoughts and feelings surrounding the situation, or do you try not to show these things?

5 I show/don't show the following thoughts and feelings:

. . . .

. . . .

6 Now answer the following important questions:

- Do your true thoughts and feelings match the messages that you are communicating to the person who is treating you badly?
- If your answer is no then ask yourself why.
- Why are you not demonstrating your true needs in this situation?
- Are you afraid of what will happen if you do express the truth?
- What is the worst thing that can happen if you stand up for yourself?
- Can you take responsibility for your experiences or do you need to blame something or someone else for what is/isn't happening in your life?
- Is it difficult to say no?
- If so why? Are you concerned that others won't like you if you say what you really mean?
- Do you care more about what people think than you do about the quality of your own life?

Now go back to the original victimizing scenario and simply alter the script. By taking an assertive approach how could you change your answers to question 2? Make sure you keep your answer in the present tense, this energizes you and begins to create your new reality.

7 I behave assertively in this situation by:

. . . .

. . . .

How does this new answer affect your other replies to the questions in
this exercise? Imagine the different scenario, see yourself in your new
role and really try to get into the being of the authentic and assertive
you; the one who is high in self-esteem. You can always use this
exercise to help you when you are finding it hard to stand your ground.
It is not always easy to face the real reasons for your circumstances,
but if you keep asking yourself those important questions all will be
revealed.

   If you find, after answering question 5, that you *are* demonstrating
your true thoughts and feelings about being put upon, then why are
you still in this situation? If you know that you are being victimized and
you *are* communicating your displeasure, and your victimizer has not
changed his/her behaviour, then you have only two choices; to stay and
be forever treated badly or to leave.

Always remember that it is *you* who have allowed yourself to be treated
in this way; there is no one else to blame. When potential victimizers
enter your life you can teach them to change their behaviour, and if
they persist in their bullying ways then you can leave. Either way you
hold all the cards; you have taken constructive control of the situation,
you have asserted yourself and have created feelings of self-respect and
high self-esteem. When you raise your game, you become a winner
because positive action always creates fresh, confident energy.

Day 4 | Review

Key Reflections for Day 4

- You were born to take on the world, so take it on!
- When you are being authentic (real and true to yourself) then your behaviour will be naturally assertive.
- We teach others the way we want them to treat us; teach them well.
- Self-belief + positive emotions + assertive action = a winning outcome.
- When your self-esteem is low then you will behave like a victim and when it is high you will behave like a winner.
- 'Victim' behaviour can be aggressive or passive or anywhere in between.
- You can, if you think you can: think it and then just do it!
- Every time you blame something or someone else you are giving away your power.
- It can be very hard to decide whether your needs come before or after the needs of someone else.
- The meaning of our actions always lies in our intention.
- By keeping in touch with your sense of humour you will avoid confusing self-awareness with endless navel-gazing.

Your 3-Point Action Plan for Day 4

1 Take any insight that you have made today:
Example: *I am always worried about other people's opinions of me and this stops me being myself.*

2 Consider any patterns (thought/emotional/behavioural) that might lie behind this:
Example: *I was bullied at school and I often struggle to believe*

that people will like me just the way I am, so I stay in a lot and haven't many friends.

3 Create an action point around a possible change of response: Example: *I am going to create a strong intention to overcome my social phobia otherwise my life will never take off. I am going to join a gym and also start a pottery class.*

Try this 3-point action plan for yourself.

My personal insights:

. . . .

. . . .

The patterns that might lie behind this:

. . . .

. . . .

. . . .

My action points:

. . . .

. . . .

. . . .

Day 5

Increase Your Self-Awareness

We shall not cease from exploration
And the end of all our exploring
Will be to arrive where we started
And know the place for the first time.

T S Eliot (poet)

Listen. Make a way for yourself inside yourself. Stop looking in that other way of looking.

Rumi (poet)

Whenever the chips are down and things aren't going so well we very often find that our self-esteem is on the line (again!). If we are feeling vulnerable, criticized, rejected or unappreciated, how can we stop ourselves falling into that downward spiral towards low self-esteem, which fast 'proves' our uselessness and worthlessness? (*See* figure 6a).

At the first hint of self-doubt you need to stop looking in that 'way of looking' and, instead, begin making 'a way for yourself, inside yourself'. In other words: *when your self-esteem is low, look to yourself for support. Look inside instead of outside.* This may be difficult at first because we are used to looking for someone to blame when things go wrong. *Blame always creates low self-esteem*; it will never enhance an experience because blame takes away our personal power. For example, if you believe that it is my fault that something has happened to you, then you have given me the power to affect your life. You have handed over the responsibility for yourself to me, you have become a victim and, by definition, you are low in self-esteem. And if you blame yourself then you will also find yourself falling down that negative spiralling path.

Figure 6a: Negative Downward Spiral

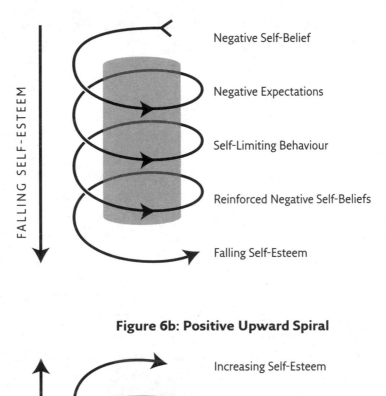

FALLING SELF-ESTEEM

Negative Self-Belief

Negative Expectations

Self-Limiting Behaviour

Reinforced Negative Self-Beliefs

Falling Self-Esteem

Figure 6b: Positive Upward Spiral

INCREASING SELF-ESTEEM

Increasing Self-Esteem

Reinforced Positive Self-Beliefs

Effective Decisive Behaviour

Positive Expectations

Positive Self-Belief

We know that positive self-beliefs create high self-esteem and negative self-beliefs create low self-esteem. Whichever view we choose as a starting point will generate a self-fulfilling prophecy and figures 6a and 6b show exactly how this works.

Imagine a day when you wake up feeling wonderful, you are confident, happy and relaxed. When you believe in yourself anything becomes possible. Because you have positive expectations you will be on the lookout for any advantageous situation which might come your way. Your behaviour will be effective and decisive, your self-esteem will increase and so you will reinforce your belief in yourself (*see* figure 6b).

Now visualize a day when things don't seem so good. You are feeling low and insecure – we all know only too well how this feels. You look out at a world where everything seems to be happening to someone else; everyone has got their life together except you. You expect the worst to happen and so it does. Even if a wonderful opportunity came your way you would either miss it or feel that you weren't good enough to take advantage of it. Your behaviour is ineffective because you can't make decisions ... and so the day goes on to prove exactly what you knew to be true. Your self-esteem falls even lower and this reinforces your original negative self-belief (*see* figure 6a).

The Magic of Self-Awareness

The positive zone is obviously the place to be, but let's not be in too much of a rush to ignore our negativity (and so throw out the baby with the bath water, as it were). In Day 1 we looked at the intimate relationship between self-dislike and low self-esteem, and it is important to remember this as we begin to shine a light on our own negative and positive patterning. It is a lot easier to acknowledge and appreciate the aspects of ourselves that we admire, than it is to recognize and embrace the ones that we don't. But we cannot change our unskilful habitual patterns unless we know what they are. Scientific research at the University of California has clearly demonstrated that the more we reinforce a pattern by repeating it, the more powerful it becomes; if we stop using a pattern, it will become increasingly weaker. So self-knowledge is crucial. We need to become familiar with our habitual responses so that we can develop those that work for us and learn to change those that don't: this information is vital to our success and happiness.

Self-awareness carries the power of transformation: it will always open your heart and mind to new levels of experience and will infuse you with fresh energy and understanding. This awareness can come as a sudden flash of insight, like a bolt from the blue, or it might be more of a slow drip, drip, drip until the penny drops; either way you will feel the change it brings. Think back to when this has happened to you. You may have caught yourself having a self-critical thought or making a negative judgment of someone and suddenly become aware of what you were doing. Perhaps you noticed a strong feeling of kindness towards a friend and realized how wonderful that was. Or you might have gained a new perspective on a situation so that you felt that you could stand in another person's shoes and really see their point of view. Every scrap of awareness is important for our development, whether we think it 'proves' how useless or how terrific we are. Stand back if you can, from self-judgment, and you will notice that *any* personal insight brings you more clarity, wisdom and confidence: you *can* understand your patterns and you *can* change them!

CONFIDENCE TIP

Recognize Your Positive Qualities

By recognizing your positive thoughts, behaviours and actions, you will enhance their effectiveness.

Examples:

I notice a feeling of gratitude and am glad of that, and this increases the strength of my original feeling.

I face a fear and hold my nerve and I can respect my courageousness.

I change a pessimistic thought for an optimistic one and realize the potential in this.

Take a look at the following positive qualities and choose three that describe you.

- Kind
- Courageous
- Warm-hearted
- Loyal
- Determined
- Passionate
- Considerate
- Friendly

- Sensitive

- Optimistic

- Thoughtful

- Helpful

- Enthusiastic

- Caring

- Loving

Take each of your three qualities and notice that by recognizing and owning them their effectiveness becomes enhanced. You can develop this even further by affirming them, saying to yourself (for example):

I am kind

I am courageous

I am warm-hearted

Nurturing Yourself

Getting to know someone else requires that there is a certain level of trust between you, and we develop this trust by nurturing the relationship. When we are trying to get to know ourselves we need this same level of commitment to the developing relationship. If I start to treat myself badly, being self-critical and blaming, the trust will be gone and the relationship will flounder. Self-awareness requires self-nurturing. But what exactly does it mean to nurture yourself?

Think of the way that you would treat a small helpless child: if she was hungry you would feed her; if she cried you would comfort her; if she made a mistake you would forgive her; if she fell over, you would pick her up and help her back to her feet. You would encourage her in every way, allowing her to make mistakes because you know that this is the only way she can learn. The child will grow because she is loved and supported; she will not learn and develop if she is abused and criticized. Of course you would treat her well because she deserves your supportive love and care.

But

- do you treat yourself in this caring way?
- do you love and nurture yourself?
- do you help yourself up when you fall, and comfort yourself when you are sad?
- do you forgive yourself when you make a mistake?

If you do all these things then you *do* know how to nurture yourself; you are your own best friend and you are high in self-awareness and self-esteem. However, it is highly probable that you don't always treat yourself in this kind and loving way. We often find it difficult to love and appreciate ourselves; it is so much easier to be self-critical. Perhaps you get angry with yourself for not being 'good enough'. Good enough for what; good enough for who? Maybe you wish that you are perfect and criticize yourself for all your imperfections. We are inclined to talk to ourselves in the same ways that people spoke to us when we were very young. Is it really any use to 'beat yourself up' about your self-perceived inadequacies/imperfections/mistakes/inabilities? Why not give yourself a break; stop telling yourself off and try some self-nurturing activities instead. Recognize your originality, celebrate your uniqueness and your stellar qualities and let yourself off the hook. As you get to know yourself and learn to love all your aspects, your self-appreciation, confidence and self-esteem will naturally blossom.

There is no one on the planet that is just like you; you are a one-off, utterly unique and original. How special does that make you feel? But of course this might not make you feel exceptional at all, especially if you are feeling low in confidence.

Stop Comparison Shopping

I coined the term 'comparison shopping' many years ago to describe one of the classic symptoms of low self-esteem, and it is a pursuit that is just as addictive as the high street variety. Comparison shopping occurs when our self-esteem is low and we begin to match ourselves against more gifted, more gorgeous and more highly intellectual others, all of whom personify total brilliance, wellbeing, confidence and charisma. As our self-worth falls, we long to escape our misery and so we look outside of ourselves for the gifts we think we lack. And naturally we find ourselves surrounded by talented and beautiful people who are all living the good life. Everyone looks more together than the way we feel. This exercise is always extremely punishing because our insecurity ensures that we inevitably find ourselves at the bottom of the pile; we are just not 'good enough' to match the unshakeable positivity and genius ability of everyone else. And if you are thinking that you don't get into this activity then think again. When you next feel inadequate, embarrassed or intimidated, just take a moment and consider this: these feelings are never just about you they are *always* about how you see yourself in relation to other people. Figure 7 shows how this works.

Comparison shopping is an emotionally driven activity. Logically, we know that we all face the ups and downs of life; no one is happy, secure and confident all the time because this is impossible. And yet when we are in the negative zone (doubting ourselves, feeling incapable and acting like a victim) we lose this rationality. Next time when negativity strikes, notice the moment before you go hurtling into comparison shopping and remember this: everything changes,

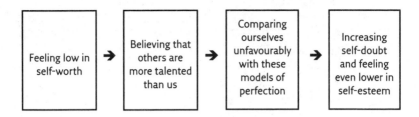

**Figure 7: The Negative Effects of
Comparison Shopping**

circumstances are unpredictable and everyone gets what they don't want sometimes. Let go of that erroneous belief that if you could only get everything right, be perfect and be 'good enough' *then* you would be safe and secure for life! Your confidence will only return when you stop running a competitive race with others (which you will always lose) and you base your relationships on co-operation and trust; when you do this you are respecting your own worth as well as the worth of others. We are all unique and remarkable in our own way and when we accept this our lives can stop being such a struggle and start to become a pretty good adventure! Try the following checklist to see how you relate to your own uniqueness and originality.

*You are the one and only you.
Be happy in your own skin and love your
uniqueness. Let yourself be yourself and
just watch your confidence levels rise.*

EXERCISE

Originality Checklist

	Answer yes or no to the following questions:	Yes	No
1	Do you love the prospect of change?		
2	Do you ever feel left out/excluded? If so, is this painful?		
3	Are you excited by new ideas?		
4	Would you describe yourself as a creative person?		
5	Do you hide in the kitchen at parties?		
6	Are you highly influenced by fashion trends?		
7	Do you feel different from others? If so is that exhilarating or not.		
8	Do you ever find yourself trying to 'fit in'.		
9	Are you an adventurous person?		
10	Have you got a sense of your own style?		
11	Do you often wish you looked like someone else?		
12	Are you upset if people don't like you?		
13	Would you describe yourself as a risk taker?		
14	Do you ever wish that you were someone else?		
15	Are you affected by celebrity culture?		
16	Your friend buys a gorgeous new pair of shoes; do you have to go and buy something as well?		

		Yes	No
17	Are you inspired by others' successes?	|	
18	Are you challenged by others' successes?	|	
19	Do you aspire to 'normality'?	|	
20	You are an exception! Do you believe that this is true?	|	

What do your answers disclose about you? People who can enjoy diversity have a more creative approach to life and relish their uniqueness rather than trying to hide it away; they are more confident than those who are always trying to 'fit in'. The words 'normal' and 'average' have no intrinsic meaning; we use these concepts in an effort to structure and compartmentalize our lives, but we need to remember that comparisons and standards are not real measurements. There is no 'normal' size of person (or bum!) or 'right' way to do anything, and if we decide to join the herd then we will be unable to reach our full potential. You will never be able to recognize and appreciate your intrinsic talents if you are trying to copy someone else. Sometimes it is very difficult to stand up and be different; why do we struggle so hard to lose our identity by attempting to be the same as others?

Our ideas and beliefs are culture-bound and indeed family-bound, because as children we learned from others around us. If we ever feel limited in some way, vulnerable, at a loss, or low in self-esteem, we *always* need to look at our beliefs; what are we believing about ourselves and our world? Where do these ideas originate? Are we trying to be the same as, be as good as, be as talented as ... who exactly? How can we judge our levels of ability, competence, awareness, cleverness? Only you can be inside you. Only you know what it feels like to be you. Only you know where you have come from and where you are going.

Everyone is facing different challenges, and a course of action which will enhance your growth may merely be a limitation to someone else. Your strengths will not be the same as mine; my weaknesses will not be the same as yours. Our self-esteem is such a precious and fragile thing, constant comparison will destroy it. To develop our inner confidence we need to give ourselves constant support and nurture, and we also need to recognize our own intrinsic, unique and amazing worthiness. When you can love your originality, enjoy your differences and feel free to be yourself you will be filled with confidence and self-esteem.

10 Ways to Celebrate Your Uniqueness

1 *Praise yourself for each success*, however small it may be. Each and every step you make is important and it is so easy to dismiss the realization of our goals by moving the goalposts further, thereby creating a situation where you are never 'good enough'.

2 *Enjoy the unique qualities of others.* Recognize that every human achievement demonstrates the incredible potential available to us all. If we run a competitive race with others we will always lose. However hard we try, there will always be someone who can improve on our performance. Learn from the achievements of others and add what you have learned to your own experience. Our human potential is incredible; enjoy the possibilities instead of being defeated by them.

3 *Enhance your originality.* Look at your differences, and instead of trying to hide them, decide to make a feature of them. The places where you feel different are where you find the keys to your personal and unique creativity. The urge to

conform destroys creativity. Whenever you feel the need to
'fit in', look carefully at what you feel are your differences and
decide to accept and embellish them; they are what make you
exceptional.

4 *Accept your aloneness.* If we celebrate our uniqueness then we
also celebrate our aloneness. Sometimes our aloneness can
be very scary. We may feel alone because no one can really
understand how we feel and 'be there' for us. It is true, no one
will ever know the inner you; you are the only person who can
know yourself. No one else can be inside you. And would you
really want anyone to know everything about you? The concept
of our aloneness carries a quality of freedom. We can release
our expectations of other people to know all about us and we
can also stop feeling guilty about not always being able to 'be
there' for others. Limiting or freeing – your aloneness can be
either of these things. By accepting your aloneness you will be
free to be yourself.

5 *Give your dreams a chance.* Have you been secretly longing to
change your life in some way and been afraid to do so? Try it,
whatever it takes. Take the risk to be different and see how
this feels. Self-esteem requires self-respect and it is hard to
respect ourselves if we are running our lives according to the
dictates of others. If there is something you long to do, give
yourself permission to begin. Life is here to be lived to the full
– give yourself a chance.

6 *Ask yourself, 'Do I really want to do this?'* whenever you find
yourself in a situation which is uncomfortable. Maybe you
are facing a challenge which you need to deal with in order to
grow. But possibly you are trying to do something which you
feel that you 'should' do and it doesn't feel right. Look inside
yourself; only you can know the answer. If it doesn't feel right
deep inside then closely examine your motives. Are you trying

to please someone else at the expense of yourself? Is it worth it? Your self-esteem is at stake.

7   *Remember your true purpose.* The wonderful motivational guru Anthony Robbins said that, 'Goals are a means to an end, not the ultimate purpose of our lives. Achieving goals by themselves will never make us happy in the long term; it's who you become, as you overcome the obstacles necessary to achieve your goals that can give you the deepest and most long-lasting sense of fulfillment.' In quest of your dreams you will face personal challenges that require you to dig deep and bounce back, again and again, and this is where you discover your inner stores of self-reliance, resilience and confidence.

8   *Be your own best friend.* Wherever you go, you take yourself, so be kind to your constant companion. And be supportive and encouraging rather than critical and invalidating. For example you might change the way you communicate with yourself, talking yourself 'up' with a friendly 'you can do it' and patting yourself on the back for all your efforts. Admire your strength of will and courageousness; you are a true inspiration to yourself.

9   *Know what you have to offer.* Think of yourself as a product that you are selling; how can you best promote yourself? What are your unique selling points? Imagine that your self-advertisement is going into the *Daily Mail* tomorrow (circulation 2.5million); now what does it say? You have 200 words to sell your talents and best features. Don't hang back here; no one needs to see this so let rip with the positive accolades. Consider past successes and personal qualities (a 'success' doesn't have to be work related or linked with material gain). Remember your social skills and inner strengths (e.g. being a good listener is a top talent!). Write this up in your journal.

10 *Be your own PR guru.* Now you are live on national TV and 5 million people are tuning in. Standing in front of a full-length

mirror (TV camera) read your ad. Feeling daft and embarrassed? Read it again. Repeat this exercise until you are projecting yourself with confidence. You will notice a change in your body language as your levels of self-esteem rise. When you project a positive self-image you really are maximizing your best asset: your unique and original self!

Consider this *Once you become aware of negative emotions you can open the door to positive change.*

Case Study

Ellen, 43, was married with three children aged 8, 10 and 15, and when we met she was working part-time as a teaching assistant at the local junior school, which two of her children attended. When we first spoke, Ellen told me that she had contacted me because she was feeling, 'demotivated, unappreciated and lacking in self-confidence'.

I asked Ellen to tell me a bit about herself and she revealed that she felt like the hub of her family's life, saying: 'They all rely on me for everything and I never really minded that until my last birthday when I suddenly thought that my own life is beginning to slip away. I used to be such a creative person and it felt like I had lost that part of me. And then, instead of just doing all the chores and fitting everything into the hours when I don't work I began to feel resentful, which was really horrible. Every time I picked up a magazine there seemed to be an article about work/life balance or how important it is to do something for you and I felt very restless and unsettled. Part of me was angry that I never had a moment for myself and the other part felt guilty that I was putting myself ahead of the family's needs and I was stuck between these two feelings. I realized that I didn't know the way forward and that even if I did I hadn't got the self-confidence to make something new happen.' And at this point Ellen finally contacted me.

When our self-esteem drops we tend to adopt a 'can't-do' rather than a 'can-do' attitude and then our self-doubt inhibits us from making new plans. When this happens we begin to lose sight of the wonderful opportunities that life can offer us and the possibility for change can then become a threatening prospect. Ellen needed to regain her self-belief and I knew that as soon as she did this, things would start moving forward for her. I asked her what she thought needed to happen first and she was quick to say that she needed to 'stop doing everything at home' and begin to delegate household duties. Those of you who have tried this will know that this is not always easy to implement, but it can be done and *has* to be done by any mum who needs a life of her own.

Once Ellen committed herself to this goal things began to change very quickly at home. Weekly rotas went up on the kitchen wall and jobs were allocated to all of the children and also to Mark her husband. Ellen was determined to get this plan off the ground and didn't let anyone get away with not doing their share. At the end of the second week she said: 'I really struggled with the temptation to give up nagging and pick up the dirty clothes off the bedroom floors, but I resisted and in the end the children had to do it themselves. After a month everyone in the family had new skills, they knew how to: fill and empty the dishwasher; separate whites and coloureds for the washing machine; use the vacuum cleaner; make me a decent cup of tea, and Mark and our eldest began cooking the evening meal.'

By the second month Ellen was feeling very different about herself. Not only had she freed up some time, but family life felt much more harmonious because, as she said, 'everyone felt like they were doing their bit and I didn't feel like a drudge'. After this, one thing led very quickly to another, and Ellen decided to follow her dream to become an English teacher. She had a degree in English and so applied to do a one-year PGCE course, which would qualify her to teach in a secondary school. We spoke again during her course and she said she felt delighted and rejuvenated, and that she was glad she had recognized her discontent when she did. She said, 'I might have just carried on not being aware of my dissatisfaction and then it would have been too late to do anything about it.'

If you are feeling disappointed or frustrated by life at the moment, don't just let it bring you down even further. Recognize that you are ready for a change and then set about discovering what sort of change that might be and how you could activate it – one easy step at a time.

Confidence is a Quality We Need to Develop

Love your life and it will love you back; this is a beautiful way of expressing the dynamics of the Law of Attraction, which states that we will attract whatever we radiate. We live within an electromagnetic field and each time we think, we charge the energy field with vibrations. Like attracts like, and so, whilst negative thought patterns attract all forms of negativity, positive thought patterns attract all forms of positivity. This means that we are not only responsible for the quality of our own consciousness but we are also responsible for our input into the collective awareness (the energetic vibes we radiate will have an effect on all other beings).

It is easier to accept our responsibility for our emotional states if we are flowing in the positive upward spiral where we are full of self-belief, feel great and can happily extend our positivity to others. The challenge lies in remembering all this when we find ourselves falling into the negative downward spiral. On a difficult day, when self-confidence is as elusive as fairy dust, we can act in our own best interests by simply reminding ourselves that we create what we are thinking about. Confident people have a healthy approach to life, which means that they can support and nurture themselves in any situation. In other

INSIGHT

Accept Yourself

How many 'yous' have you been today? You might have been *refreshed* when you woke up; *tuneful* in the shower; *rushed* on the way to work; *hassled* to get to a meeting on time; *pleased* by the appreciation of colleagues; *annoyed* and *challenged* by another colleague; *exhausted* by lunch time ... and you have only reached midday! Up and down, and up and down you go, displaying some moods and behaviour that you 'like' and some that you don't.

• Think of the emotional states that you have visited today.

Make a list of the ones you are happy to be.

. . . .

. . . .

Now consider those that you are not so happy with.

. . . .

. . . .

Are there some that you find hard to own?

The eminent psychologist Carl Rogers made a vital point when he said: 'The curious paradox is that when I accept myself just as I am, then I can change.' We cannot let go of

> what we cannot first accept; we need to be able to embrace our more difficult parts, our less attractive 'selves'. Next time you uncover a 'you' which you struggle to admire, try giving this part of you a break. Give your negative aspect a bit of your attention (perhaps you had good reason to feel angry; be intolerant; lack kindness ... etc). Let yourself off, we all have biases and prejudices and intolerances but we can't let go of them until we become aware of them and can accept them.

words, every experience becomes a chance to reach for their best and to change the negative beliefs that will inevitably arise.

Confidence is not a gift which is bestowed on some and not others; it is a quality that we develop as we increase our self-awareness and so begin to change our negative patterning. We might follow the shining example of the spiritual teacher Ram Dass, who has described himself as 'a connoisseur of my neuroses'. We all have our 'stuff' so we might just as well embrace it, and investigate it, because this is the only way towards increasing self-respect, self-appreciation, self-esteem and happiness.

Your Personal Life Performance Review

You might believe that life would be easier for you if other people could appreciate you a bit more and stop being so critical of your endeavours. Certainly it is true that we respond favourably to validation and positive feedback. And it is not only *what* is said to us that is important, but also *how* it is said. Psychologist Daniel Goleman, writing on the impact of the way that performance reviews are delivered says that, '... brain science shows that positive or negative, the way in which that review gets delivered can be a boon or a curse. If a boss gives even a good review in the wrong way, that message can be a low-grade curse, creating a neutral downer.' Goleman refers to neuroscientific research at the University of Wisconsin which shows that when we're in an I-can-handle-anything frame of mind, feeling energized by our goals, our brains turn up the activity in an area on the left side, just behind the forehead; here we function at our best. But when we are down, with no motivation and perhaps feeling anxious, our brain turns up the volume on the right side and we fall into a negative state.

Unsurprisingly, performance feedback that concentrates on what's wrong with us also sends this 'downer' brain area into overdrive. But one study showed that even the tone of delivery can trigger either area: when participants were given positive performance feedback in a cold, negative voice, they felt down even though the news was good.

This set me thinking about the importance of the tone of voice that we use to talk to ourselves. What happens to you when you consider a situation where you made a mistake or where you could have behaved with greater integrity? Do you deliver your own 'life performance reviews' in a pleasant supporting tone or are you harsh and self-critical with yourself so that you end up feeling terrible about yourself and your inabilities? You might blame others for putting you down and feeding your self-doubt, but the truth is that your harshest critic will always be yourself.

Sometimes, when I am working with a group, I stop whatever we are doing and ask everyone to think of three things that they don't like about themselves. Within minutes the job is done, everybody can think of at least three things which they are quite happy to share. And then of course I ask them to think of three things that they like about themselves. This takes much longer and many people can't even come up with one thing that they are prepared to tell the rest of us. Why is this? Why is it so much easier to bring ourselves down than raise ourselves up? Try this exercise yourself.

EXERCISE

Things I Like and Don't Like About Myself

1 Three things I don't like about myself:

....

....

....

2 Three things I do like about myself.

....

....

....

Did you find it easy to criticize yourself? Was it hard to praise yourself?

Deep down (and sometimes it's not that deep) we are all excessively self-critical; even those people who you think of as super-confident will have a well-developed inner critic. This is the name psychologists give to that fault-finding voice which delivers constant negative reviews of the way we perform in life. And if you are still wondering if this applies to you then close your eyes for a moment and just home in on all that inner activity. Day and night, hour in hour out, awake or asleep, your mind keeps doing its job: observing, evaluating, classifying, judging, ruminating ... etc. continually making inner chitchat. Actually, you are always talking to yourself and so it is most important that you get to know *what* sort of things you are saying, and also *how* you are saying them. You talk to yourself with a variety of voices and whilst one of them might be supportive and encouraging (*you can do it, keep going, you've got what it takes ...*) your inner critic will be constantly giving you messages like: *you can't do this, why bother you never stick at anything, I hate you, you don't deserve to succeed ...* . Your inner critic speaks to you from your own personal collection of all past criticisms that you have heard and believed to be true. Listen to its tone and you will probably recognize that it is one you remember from childhood.

Three important considerations:

1 Your inner critic will always keep doing its job (keep on criticizing) and it will never be satisfied.
2 This voice has no authority over you unless you give it some.
3 Your gentle self-awareness can disempower your inner critic.

The Way the Inner Critic Operates

Example
Let's take a pretty common modern dilemma and see how easily the inner critic can create a no-win situation.

> Ella decides that she will stay home and look after her pre-school child because she thinks that her daughter deserves her care and attention.

Meanwhile and at the same time she finds herself constantly bringing herself down for 'only being a housewife and a mum'.

Lisa decides to go out to work and send her young son to nursery because she wants to work, they need the money and she believes that he will enjoy the stimulation.

Meanwhile *and at the same time* she is constantly punishing herself for not being a 'good enough mother'.

Do you recognize this syndrome? It is characterized by the following qualities:

- Whichever way you decide to go you will lose.
- Confusion and guilt feature heavily.
- It will be very difficult to make decisions.
- You will feel low in self-esteem.

EXERCISE

Your Inner Critic

Think of an example of the way that the inner critic is operating in your life at the moment. Look at where you are feeling confused/guilty/indecisive/low in self-esteem. The situation will be characterized by its 'whichever way you turn you will lose' nature. Before you can let yourself off the hook (whatever it might be) you need to look carefully at the situation and try to become aware of the conflicting emotions that are involved.

On the one hand there is one possible way to act:

· ·

· ·

But there is another possible scenario:

· ·

· ·

These two possibilities are mutually exclusive. Whichever one you choose you will feel that you have made the wrong decision in some way. Shall I put my pre-school child into nursery or shall I stay at home? Either way I am not satisfied. My inner critic ensures that I will be in a dilemma however I decide to act. What can be done about this?

The key to change, development and high self-esteem is acceptance. We need to be able to accept all parts of ourselves (the good, the bad and the ugly). Accept that your inner critic will keep on nagging at you (and that only very occasionally might it have something useful to say). If you are often talking yourself down and telling yourself off, then look closely at exactly what you are saying to yourself. We know that our beliefs are not set in stone, so if they are not supporting your self-esteem then change them. Criticism is an ineffective learning tool and if you believe that you are 'not good enough' in any way then you will never have the confidence to attract success.

As soon as you start to feel low, look closely at what you believe to be true about yourself; tune into your self-talk and recognize that you have given your inner critic the authority to ruin your confidence. You are an incredible, unique and amazing person, and every time you demean yourself you are buying into an old set of negative beliefs that do not support or validate you. Recognize this to be true, release your self-criticisms, forgive your mistakes and affirm your love and support for yourself. Whenever you hear that inner critic come knocking, say the following affirmation:

Affirmation *I am doing the best I can. I am a valuable and lovable person and I deserve all the love and support that I can give myself.*

This will remind you of your true worth and, if you do need to change in any way this affirmation will give you the strength and support that you will need to make the change. When you can let yourself off all those hooks you will be free to be the creative, decisive, confident person that you really are. As you increase your self-awareness you will discover that you are so much more than you thought you were. Whenever you are looking for answers look inside yourself: you hold all the keys to the knowledge you need for your own self-development and progress. Love and value yourself, be your own kind best friend. This relationship will last forever!

Day 5 | Review

Key Reflections for Day 5

- When your self-esteem is low, look to yourself for support. Look inside instead of outside.
- The nature of your self-beliefs will generate a self-fulfilling prophecy.
- The more you reinforce a pattern by repeating it, the more powerful it becomes. And if you stop using a pattern it will become increasingly weaker.
- Self-awareness carries the power of transformation.
- By recognizing your positive qualities you will enhance their effectiveness.
- As you get to know yourself and learn to love all your aspects, your self-appreciation, confidence and self-esteem will naturally blossom.
- There is no one on the planet just like you; you are a one-off, utterly unique and original.
- Everything changes, circumstances are unpredictable and everyone gets what they don't want sometimes.
- Your self-esteem is a precious and fragile thing, and constant comparison will destroy it.
- Give your dreams a chance.
- Know and respect what you have to offer.
- Confidence is not a gift, it is a quality that you develop as you change your negative patterning.
- Become a connoisseur of your own neuroses.
- The voice of your inner critic has no authority unless you give it some.

Your 3-Point Action Plan for Day 5

1 Take any insight that you have made today:
 Example: *I have such high expectations of myself and this means that whatever I do never feels good enough and so I have no self-respect.*

2 Consider any patterns (thought/emotional/behavioural) that might lie behind this.
 Example: *My mother was hyper-critical of everything that I did; I could never make her happy.*

3 Create an action point around a possible change of response.
 Example: *I am becoming aware of when that harsh critical voice in my head starts up (sounds like my mother). I am already being kinder to myself and affirming that I am doing OK – this works!*

Try this 3-point action plan for yourself.

My personal insights:

. . . .

. . . .

. . . .

. . . .

The patterns that might lie behind this:

....

....

....

My action points:

....

....

....

Part Two

Self-Esteem For Life

Day 6

Keep Motivated

Desire is the key to motivation,
but it's the determined commitment
to an unrelenting pursuit of your goal,
a commitment to excellence, that will
enable you to attain the success you seek.

Michael Jordan (athlete)

The commitments we make to ourselves and to others,
and our integrity to those commitments, is the essence
and clearest manifestation of our procreativity.

Stephen R Covey (author)

Looking for quotes for Day 6 I realized, yet again, what a complex issue motivation really is. So often people say to me that the reason they can't go for a cherished goal is that they haven't got the motivation; they just want to know how to galvanize themselves into action. But in truth, I then wonder how 'cherished' their goal really is. I know for sure, from years and years of coaching, that when someone really wants to do something then they will find a way, and if they don't want to do something then they will find any old excuse, and 'I can't get motivated' is a popular one! I have written a lot about motivation in the past but I am beginning to think that it needs 'unpacking' in a new way if we are to really understand its multifaceted nature.

Just as we are inclined to conceptualize 'confidence' and 'happiness' as external objects (e.g. *I need more confidence, I want happiness*) we also objectify 'motivation' (e.g. *I could do it if I just had the motivation).* If we speak like this (and we all do at times) we distance ourselves from the confidence/happiness/motivation we seek, so that these qualities can seem unattainable. But we only have to remember that they are internal states of being rather than external things, and this uplifting realization puts us firmly back on track. No more wistful wonderings about the magical qualities of motivation, but a grounded understanding of how we can generate the enthusiasm, energy and commitment to obtain our goals.

Let's go back to that idea of being unable to achieve a desired goal because of lack of motivation. Perhaps this is where you find yourself right now, and if not you will undoubtedly recognize this condition because we have all been there. To have a goal and not to be able to activate it is very frustrating and confidence lowering. How often do we despair of ourselves when we are in this state: talking ourselves down (*why can't I get this together? what is the matter with me? I am such a procrastinator, I have no respect for myself ...*); writing endless to-do lists that burden us even further and plunging headfirst into that negative downward spiral of diminishing self-esteem?

Motivation Is ...

My research into this subject is extensive and I have asked many people what they think motivation involves. The following spidergram shows some of these findings. Do you relate to any of these points? Are there any others you would like to add?

Figure 8: Motivation Spidergram

Right attitude: This can encompass many things but at its root there must be commitment: to self, to your purpose, to your journey and to your goal. I love the idea of being committed to oneself; it is another good way of expressing our intrinsic self-worth.

Carrot and stick: I, personally, can relate strongly to this image and I use it quite often with clients. As our self-awareness grows we get to know ourselves very well; we understand how we operate in quest of a goal (how much we need to push ourselves on, what sort of prizes we might give ourselves along the way). I am writing this book with an extremely tight deadline which forces me to produce a certain amount of words each day. The time pressure is my stick (and it works very well) but it can also frighten me into a writing paralysis if I don't take enough breaks. So walks, cups of tea, chocolate biscuits and forays to Facebook are some of my carrots.

Focus: We know that whatever we focus on becomes our reality and so a laser beam of attention directed at our goal is a prerequisite for success. And this concentrated energy draws on our imaginative faculty so that we can start to really visualize ourselves taking the steps we need to achieve our objective. Creative visualization is a powerful manifesting tool that we are actually using unconsciously all the time – often producing unwished-for negative outcomes (e.g. if we keep 'seeing' and 'feeling' ourselves failing then this is what we will manifest).

Exciting goal: Any old goal just won't give us the juice we need. Unless we are totally and utterly in love with our objective and devoted to its outcome, we might as well not even bother to exert ourselves. Consider your passion quotient for your goal (how much you love it) scoring from 1–10 (1 being not bothered and 10 being madly, deeply …). If you score less than 10 then you will be unable to generate the motivation you will need, so just put yourself out of your misery and let it go. Remember that an exciting new goal will require effort (otherwise you would have achieved it already) and you are going to need to be right behind yourself all the way.

Enthusiasm: This word comes from the Ancient Greek meaning 'possessed by a god'; what we might call divine inspiration. And when we feel enthusiastic we are definitely in an uplifted, insightful and elevated mood. Think about when you last had this feeling and how the energy coursed through your body, generating excitement. If you are enthusiastic about your goal then this inspired energy will be just the fuel you need for the journey ahead.

Ready to leave comfort zone: Maybe it is more helpful (and less scary) to think of this as requiring 'expansion' of the zone rather than 'leaving' the security of the known. Comfort zone has two meanings: (1) A happy place where we feel secure, confident and relaxed; (2) A prison of our own making, a 'comfortable' place only because we know it so well. Actually (1) can easily morph into (2) as we change and grow and want to move on, but then find ourselves trapped by inertia born from a fear of taking a risk. A person with self-esteem knows when it is time to open up and expand their comfort zone to include more choices and possibilities. Motivation inspires personal expansion at all levels.

Positive energy: This is a definite requirement for any successful accomplishment. Emotional optimism, clear affirmations of intent and assertive action in quest of your goal all fall into this category. To remain motivated we need to be operating within the positive upward spiral of rising self-esteem, and this means embracing all the positive aspects of our energy.

Having confidence: Confidence and motivation do go hand in hand: confidence → motivation → increased confidence → stronger motivation. But remember that these are internal states and they can be generated by your strong intention to move on. If you really intend to reach your goal then you will. Sometimes you have to have the inner conviction that you can do something *even though* you don't feel confident. And it is only *after* you have taken that leap of faith that you feel confident (wow, I did it!). Don't sit around waiting for the gift of confidence to arrive before you act on your own behalf or you might wait a lifetime.

Persistence: I think that this is sometimes an underrated quality, considered rather less important than creativity, inspiration and sheer brilliance, but of course it is absolutely vital. Thomas Edison reportedly said that success is 10 per cent inspiration and 90 per cent perspiration; we start with a marvellous idea and then of course we need to make it happen. The great inventor also said that, 'Opportunity is missed by most people because it is dressed in overalls and looks like work.' What a great quote; it really says it all doesn't it?

Fearlessness: Again, this reminds us that sitting around waiting until we: are absolutely ready, have had enough training, are psychologically prepared, know we are good enough, feel more confident, are sure that we cannot fail ... etc., is a pointless waste of time (unless our objective is self-sabotage). The title of Susan Jeffers' brilliant book, *Feel the Fear and Do it Anyway*, has become an iconic message because we can all relate to the meaning behind it.

Clear goal: We have seen how a goal needs to be exciting, and just as importantly, it needs to be clear. By this I mean it needs to be specific. It is no good trying to drum up motivation for a goal that is fuzzy around the edges (or even all the way through). How will we know when we have reached our objective if it remains unspecified? Clients sometimes say that their goal is to 'be happy' or to 'be confident' but such a wide brief makes success impossible. Clarify your goal; what *exactly* do you want? When you *know* your dream and can *see* it happening, the steps you need to take will just reveal themselves before you; this is so motivating.

Wanting success: This is a real get-up-and-go generator isn't it? In relation to this book we could say that your great desire to develop confidence and high self-esteem is motivating you to keep reading. Wanting success is also closely linked to loving your goal, and the two together create an all-win emotional response.

Not procrastinating: We all know what it feels like to keep putting something off and it is most de-motivating. Procrastination can be simply an habitual reaction to anything new that might require an expansion of our comfort zone (or similar scarily demanding things). And writing endless 'to do' lists can make things even worse as we begin to overwhelm ourselves with mountainous jobs! A top tip here: throw out all those lists and concentrate on your number one priority. Take the first step towards activating this important goal. Just do this and immediately you are no longer a procrastinator!

EXERCISE

Assessing Your Own Motivation

A spidergram is a useful tool to help us make creative connections in a non-linear way. In figure 8 we used motivation as the central theme and then ideas arose that were connected to this and radiated out from it. In this exercise you simply take one of the radiating extensions in figure 8 that particularly affects your own levels of motivation, and use this as the central theme of a new spidergram; then create your own new extensions.

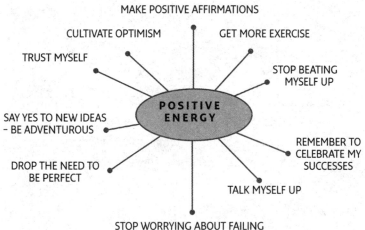

Figure 9: Your New Spidergram

You can then do the same again; taking one of your extensions and making it your central theme and so generating new extensions. This is a great way to creatively explore ideas, thoughts, feelings and actions – you can really increase your awareness of your responses and so understand how you might turn this information to your own advantage.

Get Going

Taking action in pursuit of a very short-term goal is my personal favourite motivator. Because positive action generates self-respect, then the process of simply taking one step towards a small item on your 'to do' list can really turn your energy round from apathy to enthusiasm.

Step 1 *Choose a task* that needs to be done soon or should have been done previously. This may be something that is at the back of your mind and you probably expend quite a lot of energy remembering it and then trying to forget it and then not liking yourself for not doing it ... in other words you are spending a lot of energy in the 'not doing'.

Step 2 *Decide that you will seize the moment* and do it today. As soon as you feel that rise of energy take action: pay the bill, make that phone call, mend the lamp, make an appointment for a dental check-up, pump up your bicycle tyres, phone your mum, forgive someone ...

Step 3 *Feel the benefit of your action*. It's not so much that you can ride your bike now or not worry that the water will be turned off, but rather that you have demonstrated your ability to make something happen, and that brings a great feeling of being in control again.

Step 4 *Maximize the benefits* of this wave of motivation and do something else that you have been putting off.

Step 5 *Cultivate the habit of being motivated* – decide to be enthused by life and then follow up with appropriate action.

Trust, Motivation and Self-Esteem

These three are indispensable to each other. The two quotations at the start of this chapter make the important link between motivation and commitment, and surely it is this commitment to ourselves, to others and to life itself which becomes the driving force that inspires us to reach our potential. But we can only be committed when we feel safe and we only feel safe when we can trust ourselves and the process of life.

Trust, motivation and self-esteem are part of a mutually dependent cycle which can flow either way, *see* figure 10. Flowing in an anti-clockwise direction we see that when we have self-esteem we are able to trust ourselves and the process of life, and then our motivation naturally blossoms. And flowing in a clockwise direction we can see that our self-esteem depends upon our degree of self-trust.

When you can't trust yourself you are full of self-doubt and this lack of self-belief inevitably means low self-esteem. Your degree of self-trust reflects your levels of self-respect, and if you can trust yourself then others will feel that they can trust you; they will have confidence in you. And if you feel respect for yourself then you will gain

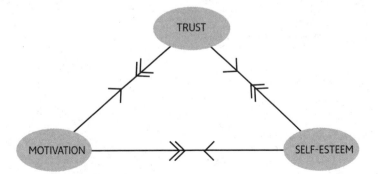

Figure 10: A Mutually Dependent Cycle

the respect of others. If you believe that you are unlovable then your relationships will reflect this belief; if you feel that you don't deserve the best in life then, for sure, you will not get the best. Perhaps you are feeling that you are just 'not good enough' for …? Try the following two-part exercise.

Action speaks louder than words and when you walk your talk your levels of self-worth and self-esteem will naturally rise.

EXERCISE

Trust Checklist

(Part 1)	Yes	No
I believe in myself		
I usually know the right thing to do		
I trust my intuition		
I give others the benefit of the doubt		
I always do the best I can		
I think that things usually work out for the best		
I learn from my mistakes		
I am safe		
The universe supports me		

Do you believe these things to be true for you? Most of our ways of thinking about ourselves and our world have been learned by us at a very early age. If your first few years of life were spent in a supportive environment and you felt well nourished (physically, mentally, emotionally and spiritually) then it is likely that you will be able to contact a sense of safety deep within you in your adulthood. If for any reason you feel that your early childhood was lacking in love and care and positive approval then you will probably find it more difficult to say and believe that 'I am safe' or that 'The universe supports me'.

(Part 2)

Go back through the checklist and think carefully about the way you answered.

1 Why did you reply the way you did?

. . . .

. . . .

2 What is difficult for you to believe and why?

. . . .

. . . .

3 What is easy for you to believe and why?

. . . .

Trust, motivation and self-esteem are inner states that depend upon each other and, in fact, help to create each other. Without self-esteem there is no trust or motivation; without motivation we lack trust and self-esteem, and without trust we lack both self-esteem and motivation. The positive take on this is that once we recognize a tendency to be low in any of these three states we can work on either of the other two in order to raise our game.

---

10 Ways to Get Super-Motivated

1 *Ditch the 'armchair contemplation'.* When you think and think about doing something it can really feel like you are getting on with it but unfortunately this is not the case. There comes a time when thinking must be converted to action.

2 *Make a list/cull your lists.* If being orderly is not your style, then introducing some structure to the chaos might be just what you need. On the other hand, if you are surrounded by lists then the sheer number of jobs will defeat you. Identify your top three priorities and let that be your only list.

3 *Accept that you are not perfect.* If you don't, you will be unable to get going because whatever you do will never feel 'good enough'.

4 *Trust yourself.* Remember past successes and achievements. Recollect some good decisions you have made. You have followed through for yourself in the past and you can do it again.

5 *Consider the carrots!* Think of the rewards of getting going; what will it feel like to have completed the task? How pleased will you be?

6 *Stick to the knitting.* This old phrase says it in a nutshell. Once

you have made the commitment to act, stick with it and keep going, do whatever needs to be done. Feel the self-respect!

7   *Act confidently.* Step up to the plate, even if you are feeling unsure. A courageous leap will energize, motivate and enthuse you – just do it!

8   *Stop waiting to feel in the right mood.* Days, weeks and months can pass while you wait to feel ready to act. You might never feel ready, particularly if the task hasn't got a passion quotient of 10/10; meanwhile the pressure mounts.

9   *Become aware of your excuses.* What strategies do you use to subvert your goals? Realize that they just won't wash any more.

10 *Take the decision to be motivated.* Let this strong intention override all your apparent inner and outer obstacles. Act as if you are motivated and you will feel motivated – be the change you seek.

Waiting to be motivated is a complete waste of time because motivation is an 'inside job'. You simply create a strong intention to act and then follow it through, it is as simple as that.

Raising Self-Esteem, Developing Trust and Increasing Motivation – Using Cognitive Therapy

I love this extract from *The Pooh Book of Quotations* by AA Milne:

> The old grey donkey, Eeyore stood by himself in a thistly corner of the forest, his feet well apart, his head on one side, and thought about things. Sometimes he thought sadly to himself, 'Why' and sometimes he thought, 'Wherefore?' and sometimes he thought, 'Inasmuch as which?' and sometimes he didn't quite know what he was thinking about.

I used this quotation in my book *Fast Track to Happiness*, and although I searched for something else to use here I couldn't find anything as eloquent as this piece. It is so funny and so sad at the same time, and everyone can relate to it at the very deepest level. It speaks to all those who have ever found themselves standing in a thistly corner (and that certainly includes us). And just like Eeyore, we can let our chattering mind take us along those dark and dreary paths leading towards anxiety, worry and self-doubt. How often have you found yourself not knowing what you are thinking? When we are unconscious of the nature of our thoughts we are at the mercy of our mental processes and then, like Eeyore, we feel lost, adrift and out of control.

We have looked at the CBT model (showing the interdependency of our thoughts, feelings and behaviour) in earlier chapters, where we discovered that thoughts are not facts. Here we apply this simple practical formula again. Cognitive therapists recognize that the nature of our reality is far from fixed and that it is actually the by-product of our own perceptions; specific errors in thinking create specific problems, and more skilful thoughts lead to happier outcomes. This is the theory behind the process:

A (event) → B (thoughts about event) → C (emotions resulting
from thought
processes)

Now look at this example:

A (I lose my job) → B (I think I am useless, no one will
ever employ me again) → C (I feel unmotivated and low in
self-esteem)

Using the principles of cognitive therapy we can lift our confidence
levels and get the motivation needed to apply for another job. We do
this by examining the truth of our thoughts. In the example above I
could challenge the belief that I am useless and that no one will employ
me again; these thoughts are based on what are called 'cognitive distortions' and they are taking me down into the negative spiral of low
self-esteem. If I am rational I can see that I am massively overreact-
ing and this realization opens up all my positive possibilities: a more
confident mood, a new optimistic approach and the motivation to take
action on my own behalf.

Psychologist Aaron Beck suggested that lack of motivation and
ongoing sadness are the outcome of cognitive distortions, which are
based on specific beliefs about the world, the future and ourselves. For
example, if I have trust issues I will tend to be suspicious of others,
finding it hard to be relaxed and believe in a friendly and abundant
universe. And if I have little self-worth I won't have the confidence to
follow through and achieve my goals.

EXERCISE

Change Your Mind to Change Your Mood

You can use this A → B → C formula when you are trying to unravel your own internal processes in reaction to any testing situation. Challenge any negativity by investigating your 'evidence' thoroughly.

Choose a difficult event (A) then complete B and C.

Example

Step 1	(A) Event	My partner leaves me.
Step 2	(B) Thoughts	I am no good at relationships because I am such a horrible, worthless person.
Step 3	(C) Emotions	I am angry; am full of self-dislike; can't trust myself; lack confidence; have no motivation etc.
Step 4	Test (B)	Ask yourself if these thoughts are really true? Have you concrete examples that prove your worthlessness? Have you evidence of your horribleness?

When we reflect on our reactions to any stressful situation we often find that our immediate thoughts are based on 'cognitive distortions' rather than on reality. We can then insert a more realistic reaction at stage B, which leads to an uplift of emotions and a more positive result.

INSIGHT

You May Not Be Perfect But Nevertheless ...

Sometimes the need to be 'perfect' is simply the result of our trying to do the best we can and then just expecting far too much of ourselves. The quest towards perfectionism can then push us into a tight corner where we can't move for fear of proving our 'inadequacies'. There is a way out of this dilemma.

- Take a realistic look at what you consider to be a weakness of yours or a mistake you have made. Use concrete examples. For instance:

A weakness – *I am not up to speed with the computer skills I need for my job.*

A mistake – *I gossiped about a friend of mine and I shouldn't have done that.*

- Choose a quality of yours that helps to balance out your perceived weakness, e.g. *I am good at networking and I am approachable at work.*

- Do the same for your mistake, e.g. *I haven't done this before, I am a good friend.*

- Now link the two sentences with the words, *but nevertheless...* So the weakness example would read:

I am not up to speed with the computer skills I need for my job **but nevertheless** *I am good at networking and I am* *approachable at work.*

The mistake example would read:

I gossiped about a friend of mine and I shouldn't have done that **but nevertheless** *I haven't done this before, I am a good friend.*

Mistakes and weaknesses, we all have them, and we have strengths and qualities too. Next time you apply your strict standards of perfection to yourself remember that this is an unrealistic and inhibiting strategy which will only result in a loss of confidence and motivation.

Be mindful of this truth today:

I may not be perfect **but nevertheless** *I ...*

Consider this: *If you still can't raise the motivation for that exciting goal then it is highly likely that you are harbouring unrealistic fears.*

Case Study

Michelle, 49, worked on the checkout at a well-known supermarket. She is married to Dave and their three grown-up children had flown the nest. They had lived in a London suburb for 25 years and had a comfortable lifestyle. But Michelle was bored and read an article about me in a magazine and decided to have some coaching to 'clear her head' (her words). Some clients have a particular issue to work on and they know what it is, but most often people tell me they just want to 'get clear about what they want'. There is so much talk about 'going for our goals' and 'achieving our outcomes' but for much of the time we just keep going in the same old way, following our well-worn routines, day in day out, without much thought about taking a new direction. Sometimes a tragedy or crisis brings us face to face with our mortality and suddenly we want to move out of our comfort zone and expand our horizons. Or maybe we just feel restless, disenchanted or bored. Either way we have come to a crossroads and are ready for a change.

Michelle told me that she and Dave had often talked about moving to the countryside to set up a market gardening enterprise and he was full of plans of how to set about this. They ran two allotments and he worked at a garden centre; he had always wanted to run his own business one day. His father had left them some money and they were now free to move, but although Michelle felt bored by her routines she resisted the idea and Dave couldn't understand why. She wanted to speak to me about what she called her 'options'. As we talked, it became clear that she had many unexpressed fears about realizing the market gardening dream and was confused about what she felt.

I have a really great exercise called *The Best and Worst Case Scenarios*, and I use it to help clients to name realistic fears and weed out the unrealistic ones, so I gave this to Michelle to do. It has five stages and it might be something that you will find useful too.

Michelle used this exercise to structure her thoughts and feelings, and she said: 'I found it very helpful to get it all down in black and white instead of just having muddled thoughts going round and round in my head; it gave me some perspective and Dave and I could then discuss what I had written.' When she did this exercise Michelle realized what an amazing opportunity this could be for the two of them. Dave was thrilled that she was considering it seriously and the more they talked about it the more enthusiastic she felt. Yes, she had fears based around moving away from friends and her job. She also expressed concern over money, although admitted that Dave had written a detailed financial plan for the venture and had a good head for business. But in the end the excitement of creating a new enterprise together overruled her worries and they decided to look for a suitable property.

You can use this exercise in any situation where you would like to weigh up your conflicting feelings. For example, you might be concerned that stepping into your confident shoes might rock the boat; but is that such a bad thing? Others might not like your new plans; is that enough to stop you moving forward? Your enterprise might fail but would that really be the end of the world? Confidence and self-belief are the gifts you get when you are prepared to take a motivated (but calculated) leap into your new future! Why not test this hypothesis?

If your dream is big enough and exciting enough you will be enthused by all the energy and stamina you need.

EXERCISE

The Best and Worst Scenarios

Stage 1 Think of a change you might make, anything new you are considering or a specific goal and name it.

My goal is
....

Stage 2 Now imagine achieving the goal; what would be the best-case scenario?

The best possible outcomes would be
....

Stage 3 Consider the worst possible scenario.

The worst possible outcomes would be
....

....

Stage 4 In what ways, if any, do your anxieties and fears help or hinder you?

....

....

Stage 5 Name any fears and anxieties that you would like to overcome.

....

....

Day 6 | Review

Key Reflections for Day 6

- If you objectify motivation, confidence and happiness, you distance yourself from these qualities and they become unattainable.
- To have a goal but be unable to activate it is very confidence-lowering and frustrating.
- Creative visualization is a powerful manifesting tool that we are actually unconsciously using all the time.
- If you are enthusiastic about your goal then this inspired energy will be just the fuel you need for the journey ahead.
- Motivation inspires personal expansion at all levels.
- Don't sit around waiting for the gift of confidence to arrive before you act on your own behalf, or you might wait a lifetime.
- Being motivated is a state of mind.
- You can change your mind to change your mood.
- Your commitment to yourself, to others, and to life itself becomes the driving force that will inspire you to reach your potential.
- The nature of our reality is actually a by-product of our own perceptions.
- You may not be perfect but nevertheless you have many positive qualities.

Your 3-Point Action Plan for Day 6

1 Take any insight that you have made today:
Example: *I find it hard to trust myself to stick to a plan and see it through.*

2 Consider the patterns (thought/emotional/behavioural) that might lie behind this:
Example: *I let myself give up on things when I feel too challenged and then I lose even more motivation.*

3 Create an action point around a possible change of response.
Example: *I think my goals are often unrealistic. I am going to create a short-term goal that won't be too hard to accomplish just so that I can show myself that I can stick at things.*

Try this 3-point action plan for yourself.

My personal insights:

. . . .

. . . .

. . . .

The patterns that might lie behind this:

. . . .

. . . .

....

....

My action points:

....

....

....

....

Day 7

Practise the Happiness Habit

To a happy person, the formula for happiness is quite simple: Regardless of what happened early this morning, last week, or last year – or what may happen later this evening, tomorrow, or three years from now – now is where happiness lies.

Richard Carlson (author)

Day 7 | Practise the Happiness Habit

It has been said that if you do something for twenty-one days, without fail, it will become a habit, a ritual in your life. Most people spend time trying to change or break habits. You may not have spent time practicing obtaining a habit, but the habit of happiness is one that is worth practicing.

Dr Robert M Sherfield (author)

This is an interesting thought isn't it? I can really relate to the pre-occupations involved in changing or breaking negative habits, and it is such a wonderful and uplifting turnaround to decide instead to *adopt* a new habit; it sounds a lot easier for a start. But before we investigate the ins and outs of practising the happiness habit, here is a story.

You may have heard of some of the humorous exploits of the 13th-century Sufi philosopher Mulla Nasrudin, which have been immortalized in the work of Idries Shah. This is one of his Nasrudin tales.

A man is walking home late at night when he sees a worried Mulla Nasrudin down on all fours, crawling in the road, madly searching under a streetlight for something on the ground.

'Mulla what have you lost?' the passer-by asks.

'I am searching for my key,' Nasrudin says worriedly.

'I'll help you look,' the man says and starts searching with Mulla Nasrudin. Soon they are both down on their knees under the streetlight looking for the key. Eventually the man says, 'Tell me Mulla, do you remember exactly where you dropped your key?'

Nasrudin waves his arm back towards the darkness and says, 'Over there, in my house. I lost the key inside my house ... .' Shocked and exasperated, the passer-by jumps up and shouts at Mulla Nasrudin, 'Then why are you searching for the key out here in the street?'

'Because there is more light here than inside my house,' Mulla Nasrudin replies nonchalantly.

Of course we want to feel good, we all want the key to happiness, and this is a wish that we share with all other beings. But, as the tale suggests, we might do well to check out where we are looking for this key. When I wrote my book, *Fast Track to Happiness*, I uncovered some interesting research undertaken by psychologists at the Universities of California, Missouri and Illinois.

Their study showed that happy people are greater achievers and more successful in both their relationships and their careers, than those with a more miserable approach. The researchers discovered this was because the happier that people were, the more they were inclined to welcome new experiences and challenges and to go for new goals. Their positive moods also made them more energetic, outgoing and popular – qualities that also helped them to do well. The results showed that the more cheerful people are inclined to have happier marriages, to earn more and also to outlive their more miserable peers. These interesting findings contradict the widely held assumption that having the right job, a great partner or more money, necessarily *leads* to happiness. Dr Sonja Lyubomirsky, who led the study, said: 'Our review provides strong support that happiness, in many cases, leads to successful outcomes, rather than merely following from them.'

And so, back to the Mulla Nasrudin story. Perhaps the question we need to be asking ourselves is, 'Am I searching in the right place for the keys to my happiness?' When clients talk to me about their goals, and I ask them why their success is important, they invariably say that it is because it will make them happy. But maybe we are looking at this the wrong way round; it appears that if we make happiness our aspiration then all the rest might just drop into place.

In 1998 Professor Martin Seligman began a new psychological movement with the central idea that psychology should be focusing on the positive habits that create happiness, rather than on focusing on the negative states which lead to unhappiness. This new Positive Psychology (also called the science of happiness) had its roots in research that showed that childhood experiences and genetic traits account for only 50 per cent of our happiness potential and that we have control of the rest. It has also been shown that those who describe themselves as 'very happy' are no more beautiful, sociable or successful than the average person. The social scientists claim that the vital difference between us being happy or unhappy depends on whether we have taken two essential steps:

Step 1 We have discovered what makes us happy.
Step 2 We have included more of these happiness-making
activities in our lives.

You might be thinking that this is hardly rocket science, and I do agree, it does sound just like common sense. But take a moment here to think about how you relate to these two steps.

Acquiring the Happiness Habit

Step 1 sounds so easy but may pose a number of questions. Are you clear about what makes you happy? If you find yourself in that downward negative spiral right now then this question is hard to answer. Low self-confidence makes us miserable, and when we are in this state we can hardly remember what it feels like to be happy, let alone how to generate any get-up-and-go energy. You might be doing things to keep someone else happy or you may be struggling with your inner pessimist, awash with self-doubt or unable to focus on positive goals. And although we all deserve to be happy you might not be feeling this at the moment. Perhaps you have some old beliefs about happiness that are holding you back or maybe you are facing a difficult challenge right now. Check out where you are starting from in the happiness stakes.

QUIZ

How Happy are You?

Read the following statements and ask yourself if they are true for you.

Score as follows:
1 always   2 often   3 sometimes   4 rarely   5 never

		Score
1	I know how to have fun.	
2	I believe that I deserve the best that life has to offer.	
3	I make time to do what gives me most pleasure.	
4	I have good personal boundaries.	
5	I have an optimistic approach.	
6	I like and respect myself.	
7	I know my strengths and qualities.	
8	I enjoy good relationships with others.	
9	I have a good work/life balance.	
10	I am positive and motivated.	

If you scored 10–20

You are feeling pretty good about life and are already practising the habit of being happy. This is the score of a person who actively seeks to stay in the positive upward spiral of high self-esteem. Flexible and balanced, you have a developed sense of self-awareness and you can appreciate all your efforts in spite of your mistakes. As you move on in your journey you will experience even more subtlety in your understanding of what it really means for you to be happy. Keep doing what you are doing!

If you scored 21–30

This range of scores demonstrates someone with intimate self-knowledge. You are aware of the way you relate to the positive upward spiral of increasing self-esteem and the downward spiral en route to low self-esteem. However, you do not always use your insights to your best advantage and there are times when you are not wholeheartedly behind yourself. Start to become mindful of the moments when you sabotage your happiness and confidence, and do this kindly; you are looking to help yourself here, not to criticize yourself even further. Gather evidence and knowledge of the negative patterns and defensive habits that stand in the way of your happiness and then you can begin to let them go.

If you scored 31–40

A score at the lower end shows that you are a person who also has a lot of self-knowledge. Sometimes you are inclined to rebel against what you know does you good, and this naturally leads to feelings of low confidence and unhappiness. Perhaps you even ask yourself why you do this. Stop asking yourself and simply adopt the positive psychology line: concentrate on what makes you happy and not what makes you unhappy.

A score at the upper end demonstrates an underlying feeling of being undeserving. This is sometimes a key that unlocks hardcore negativity (patterns that seem to have us in their grip). Start to remind yourself that you are a wonderful person who *does* deserve the best; keep at this and you will begin to believe it.

If you scored 41–50

You are reading the right book! There is not such a huge chasm between those who are happy and those who are not. High self-esteem is not a special gift given to the lucky few. Self-esteem and happiness are inner qualities that we can develop for ourselves; don't forget this. You have all the tools you need as well as the most important quality of all – you are motivated to change. This strong intention led you to this book and all you have to do is to implement these daily strategies. Take one step at a time and practise the techniques, remaining kind to yourself throughout. If your goal is to increase your levels of self-esteem and happiness then you can easily achieve this; just keep going.

10 Ways to Catch the Happiness Habit

Happiness, like anxiety, is contagious. Here are some of my favourite ways to 'catch' happiness:

1 *Do something fun and frivolous* – you are guaranteed to capture some carefree childlike energy.
2 *Slow down and 'smell the roses'.* Try this when you next find yourself rushing madly from pillar to post and recognize how it feels to stop and take a breather – you deserve it.
3 *Stay in the moment.* Try this now by bringing all your attention to this very instant. We burden ourselves with anxieties about the future and regrets and recriminations about the past – let them go and step into the NOW now!

4 *Appreciate, appreciate and then appreciate some more.* A self-explanatory top tip, begin this immediately.

5 *Sing in the shower* and start the day with a wonderful lifting of the spirits.

6 *Perform an act of kindness*, and you will definitely catch some happy vibes.

7 *Be glad for this day.* You are a unique and incredible human being, make the most of your opportunities.

8 *Smile, smile, smile.* The physical act of smiling triggers a rise of endorphins (otherwise known as happiness hormones).

CONFIDENCE TIP
Take the Path With a Heart

Jack Kornfield is trained in clinical psychology and is an ordained Buddhist monk. In his famous book, *A Path with Heart*, he says, 'We must make certain that our path is connected to our heart ... When we ask, "Am I following a path with heart?" we discover that no one can define for us exactly what our path should be ... If we are still and listen deeply, even for a moment, we will know if we are following a path with heart.'

Whenever you are not feeling at your best, take a moment and check the nature of your path. On a path with heart:

• You feel motivated and positive.

• There is a deep sense of 'rightness' about what you are doing.

• You are inspired to act in a certain way.

9 *Be wholehearted about whatever you do.* If a thing's worth doing, it's worth doing properly. My dad was always saying this to me when I was a child and now I know how right this is. Give yourself to life and life will love you back.

10 *Celebrate your successes.* How often we rush on to the next thing, moving the goalposts as we go. When you can stop and recognize your achievements you nourish your feelings of self-respect and happiness.

- It is a pathway full of kindness.

- Things seem to 'flow' fairly easily and smoothly.

- Others are supportive.

- It feels like the universe is on your side.

Apply these points to test any difficult situation you are facing right now.

For example, imagine that you are making a career choice and are feeling uninspired and anxious, even though others are being supportive. Obviously your heart is not in this and you need to question your decision. When your actions don't fit with a heartfelt confidence then it is time to review your situation. Often we change on the inside and then find that we have 'outgrown' our circumstances and they just don't 'fit' any more. When this happens we are at another one of life's crossroads and just need to check the way our heart feels that we should go, and then follow that path.

Happiness is a Decision

'Don't worry be happy' can be such an annoyingly patronizing piece of advice can't it? It is just a meaningless cliché when we are miserable. Whilst at the other end of the spectrum is the darkness and misery surrounding the relatively newly named syndrome called GAD. Scientists have 'discovered' Generalized Anxiety Disorder; something else for us to get anxious about then! Happy clappy, or doom and gloom; which way to go? Life can be hard, it's true, and we need a workable strategy when we are feeling down; clichés and scary syndromes will not do it for us. We know that we increase our happiness quotient by focusing on the positive qualities and habits that lift our spirits, and that concentrating on negativity will only make things feel worse. It has been said that happiness is a decision; in other words it is an ongoing attitude, a wonderful way to view the process of our life. Let's see how making a decision to be glad (rather than buying into the hopelessness of GAD) can raise our confidence, self-respect and motivation.

Being positive does not mean taking a simplistic and naïve approach to life. On the contrary, positivity is always life affirming, realistic and constructive; it is an uplifting quality that lightens our mood and enlightens our behaviour – as they say, what is there not to like? I can choose my view of the world: my glass is half empty or half full; my cake is half gone or there's half left; I believe that I make things happen or that things just happen to me; I get worried about how stressed I am or I turn my mind to pleasanter thoughts.

Lionel Ketchian is a writer and presenter, and a tireless advocate of the happiness phenomenon. He runs the Happiness Club, a worldwide organization which promotes the benefits of being happy through meetings, newsletters and a website www.happinessclub.com. In one of his newsletters Lionel says that:

'Being happy is my most important job. All you need is the desire to be happy. There is no other way to be happy than to understand how to do it or to have someone show you how. Happiness is a learned response ... Happiness must be premeditated. You can't find it out there! You have to bring it with you. When you practice premeditated happiness, you go into every situation bringing your own happiness with you. You have your own reservoir to dip into. You don't have to look for it; you just need to practice being happy.'

He reminds us that we can't find happiness outside of ourselves; money, sex, chocolate, new shoes ... all rather lovely I admit, but none of them can bring lasting contentment. And I love this idea that we can bring our own happiness with us; it is so empowering and confidence inducing. Of course things go wrong, naturally we worry and fret, but we don't need to let these natural reactions force us into that negative downward spiral. Instead we can dip into our own reservoir of happiness, which includes our positivity, stamina, bounce-back-ability, and decision-making powers. Let's see how this might work.

Imagine your own reservoir of happiness –
a calm and joyful resource that you can dip
into at any time. How wonderful it feels to
know that this supply is only a thought away.

EXERCISE

Stopping Stress Getting to You

The next time a difficulty arises and you can feel your stress levels mounting, do the following:

Step 1 *Make the happiness decision*, which is really shorthand for: recognizing your reaction; remembering that you can choose to sink or swim and deciding to take a positive approach.

Step 2 *Take a positive approach* to your anxiety. Stress is a happiness buster as well as a health hazard, so don't pile on the worrying and compound your concern. Acknowledge that you are only experiencing a feeling of being unable to cope (remind yourself that we all feel like this sometimes).

Step 3 *Make a realistic assessment of the situation*. This means looking directly at why you feel you can't cope.

Step 4 Ask yourself what you can do to resolve the situation. If there is nothing you can do then let it go. And if you can do something then make an action plan.

Step 5 *Make a list of the actions you need to take*. Then act, taking one simple step at a time. As you work towards resolving your dilemma you will regain control and feel more confident, and all because you made the happiness decision.

Consider this: *A deep underlying emotional pattern can sabotage all the hard work you are doing to increase your self-esteem and happiness.*

Case Study

Nick, 39, is an investment banker whose girlfriend Sarah bought him some life coaching with me for a birthday present. At first he was reluctant to talk, as he was doubtful that coaching could help him in any way, but in the end decided he had nothing to lose by giving it a try. Sometimes the clients that have reservations are the ones that most benefit from coaching, once they discover that they can use me as a useful sounding board. Nick talked about what he called his 'boring pattern of giving up and feeling stressed when something good happened'. He said that Sarah was fed up with his negative attitude, which she noticed most when things were going well for him. She had bought my book, *Weekend Life Coach*, and he had read it and realized that this negative pattern was limiting his happiness.

We spent two sessions really scrutinizing this pattern and also considered its roots. Our unconscious patterning needs to be made conscious so that we can see exactly *how* we are operating and *why* we keep repeating this (even though it is clearly doing us no good). I asked him to give me a real example of how he has sabotaged himself by falling into a negative downward spiral when something good has just happened. He said that the last time he did this was recently when he and Sarah announced their engagement; 'I began to feel strange during the [engagement] party and by the end of it I was totally freaked out and thought that we were making a terrible mistake. I fell into a complete slump and took some time off work, it was then that Sarah suggested I talked to you.'

It was obvious that his reaction was not based on any real fears – he had proposed to Sarah and they had lived happily together for five years. And he knew his reaction was highly irrational and that when good things happen he tended to get scared. He eventually told me about a tragedy that occurred when he was four and his brother was six. They were on a family seaside holiday when his brother drowned in the sea and he felt that the family was still experiencing the fallout from this. Nick said that from the day of his brother's death until now, 36 years later, he was on red alert whenever the going got good and he related it to this incident.

We devoted a number of sessions to Nick's grief and all the mixed feelings that are part of the grieving process, and we also discussed how his parents overprotected him as a result of the tragedy. He could easily see how he had quickly become a little boy who had learned to be afraid, and especially to be afraid on potentially happy occasions. He said, 'I think at some deep level I believe that if I can stop a good thing happening then I will be preventing an inevitable tragedy.' There was no quick fix for Nick but things improved as soon as he was able to be aware of his fearful and concerned feelings *as they occurred* in the midst of a joyful or successful occasion. Eventually he learned to meditate and this played an important part in helping him to detach himself from the pattern.

How Happiness and Self-Esteem Go Together

Happiness is an inside job rather than something we can go out and get. Take a look at figure 11 to see just some of the ways that a person expresses and creates happiness. You will notice that these 'happiness' habits could also be called 'self-esteem' habits: happiness and self-esteem go together like the moon and the stars on a clear night. However, don't let's get bogged down and overawed by all these virtues – they are aspirational rather than actual; we are a work in progress, and we embrace these qualities when we can.

Figure 11: Happiness as an Inside Job

Our degree of happiness is directly affected by our levels of self-esteem, and on days when our self-worth is low we will definitely find ourselves carrying miserable thoughts. We might not even be conscious that we are doing this. Positive affirmations (sometimes called mantras) are the perfect antidote to negativity because they challenge the validity of our unhappy beliefs in the most immediate way. And don't worry if you just cannot believe your new positive affirmations because actually that is the whole point; they *absolutely contradict* your negative beliefs. Of course you will find it hard to believe them, but you must practise believing them so that you change your thinking habits and so change your mood.

EXERCISE

Think Happy Thoughts About Yourself

Self-help guru Dr Wayne Dyer says: 'When you change the way you look at things, the things you look at change.' Consider how your opinions and views of yourself and others could be affecting the quality of your life. Make a list of any of your thoughts, beliefs and ideas that might be hindering your happiness and success. Then take this list of negative affirmations and turn them around so that they become positive. The following example demonstrates how to do this.

Negative Affirmation	becomes	Positive Affirmation
I am a quitter	→	I always follow through
I am useless	→	I am good enough
I am lazy	→	I can apply myself
I can't say no	→	I can express my feelings
I always mess up	→	I do the best I can
I hate myself	→	I can appreciate my qualities
Things never work out for me	→	I am in control
I am a loser	→	I am a winner

Keep your affirmations in the present tense because if you say that 'I will be ... ' it will never be realized, it will remain a future promise. And for maximum impact you need to give this strategy the benefit of the doubt. For example, if your negative affirmation was, *I am a useless decision-maker* and you change this for *I make great decisions*, stay with the feeling that comes with this new belief, rather than remembering all the times you have been indecisive. Don't look for evidence to disprove a positive affirmation, rather, just *get into the reality of it and imagine it is true for you* and as you do so your feelings about yourself and your actions will fall into line with the new belief: if you *feel* decisive then you will be able to *act* decisively, it really is as easy as that.

But it's no good approaching this half-heartedly; you will not feel like a winner just because you said 'I am a winner' this morning when you got up. Your *mind* needs consistent reminding; you need to change those harmful old habits by creating some new ways of thinking, and this takes some application. I have affirmations stuck up on my office wall and on cards in my pocket, bag and briefcase and in my car. I sing positive mantras whilst gardening, showering, driving, cooking, writing ... I probably even do this in my sleep! I am always working at maintaining my PMA (positive mental approach) because I need to keep reminding myself to be positive, otherwise, at the first hint of a difficulty I would just seamlessly slip into that downward negative spiral. Training our minds to be positive is essential for our happiness and self-esteem.

INSIGHT

Be Here Now

- Come right back from wherever your mind has taken you – to the future for a quick plan or worry, or to the past for a nostalgic look or a regretful ruminate. Enter into this precious moment of your life, exactly where you are right now, this perfect moment of peace.

- Notice your breathing, in, out, in, out, in, out ... and then, before you know it, there you are again musing and plotting about the future, or looking back into the past.

- Return mindfully to the present each time you notice yourself being distracted.

Zen master and peace activist Thich Nhat Hanh describes a simple and effective way for us to anchor ourselves in the now. He says: 'Breathing in, I calm body and mind. Breathing out, I smile. Dwelling in the present moment I know this is the only moment.'

Conscious breathing is a technique that you can use anywhere at any time. Try this in any challenging situation today and notice how it changes your perspective. Use it when you find yourself lost in past or future imaginings (fantasies). Take a mindful walk, remaining conscious of your breathing for as long as you can and gently returning your focus each time your mind drifts off. Experience the perfect pleasure of some happy mindful moments, free of anxiety and free of thoughts.

Day 7 | Review

Key Reflections for Day 7

- You might need to check that you are looking in the right place for your happiness.
- In many cases happiness leads to successful outcomes rather than following from them.
- When in doubt about an action, ask yourself this question: 'Am I following the path with a heart?'
- Both happiness and anxiety are contagious; be sure to catch the happiness habit.
- Appreciate, appreciate and then appreciate some more – you are guaranteed to create happy vibes.
- Happiness is a learned response, you can't find it 'out there'; you have to bring it with you.
- You will not always be able to feel positive and happy and high in self-esteem, but embrace these qualities whenever you can.
- Your opinions and views become a lens through which you filter your perceptions. By replacing your negative affirmations with positive ones you create new realities.
- Training your mind to be positive is essential for your happiness and self-esteem.
- When you dwell in the present moment you will know that it is the only moment.

Your 3-Point Action Plan for Day 7

1 Take any insight that you have made today:
Example: *I have only just realized that I live in the future. I am always planning and making lists, which wears me out and makes me unhappy; I never feel 'on top' of things.*

2 Consider the patterns (thought/emotional/behavioural) that might lie behind this:
Example: *I write lists to help me feel in control but this isn't working. I keep moving mentally and physically but it stresses me out because I am on an endless treadmill.*

3 Create an action point around a possible change of response:
Example: *I am going to cultivate the habit of conscious breathing. I love the idea of going on a mindful walk and I know that slowing down and learning to appreciate some of my moments will make me calmer and happier.*

Try this 3-point action plan for yourself.

My personal insights:

. . . .

. . . .

. . . .

The patterns that might lie behind this:

. . . .

. . . .

. . . .

My action points:

. . . .

. . . .

. . . .

Day 8

Attract Success

All you need to know is the future is wide open and you are about to create it by what you do.

Pema Chödrön (Buddhist nun, teacher and author)

This we all know: all things are connected like the
blood that unites one family. All things are connected.
Whatever befalls the earth befalls the sons of earth. Man
did not weave the web of life. He is merely a strand on it.
Whatever he does to the web he does to himself.

Chief Seattle of the Suquamish Native American tribe

A much quoted piece and easy to see why; it is such a beautiful reminder that our awareness of the interconnectedness of all things opens our hearts and minds to our true potential.

Long before I had ever heard about the Law of Attraction and *way* before the notion of Cosmic Ordering entered the self-help genre, I was operating with a rather neat philosophy that seemed to work well for me. I think I had a lucky start, with parents who were (and still are) very positive in their outlook; I learned to assume that the best would happen for me, and by and large it has. And now I know how this has come about. Things are not what they seem to be. Nobel Laureate Max Planck discovered that everything in existence vibrates and, at a subatomic level, all matter is energy. Look at your foot, the curtains, the sky through your window, this page, the wall; all these objects look different and separate from each other, but this is just an illusion. In fact the basic building blocks of your foot and curtains and the sky, page and wall (and everything else you can see) are identical. Your body is made of the same substance as your cat, the moon, a butterfly, a gorilla, your lover, a biscuit, your enemy and this book. Take a few moments to reflect on this.

And there is more; this seemingly 'solid' world is not at all solid because everything that exists is made entirely of atoms, each of which consists of a tiny nucleus, with a very few tiny particles, called electrons, orbiting around it. Atoms are in fact energy fields having positive, negative and neutral charges and they produce electric and magnetic forces. And so our universe is a huge ocean of vibrating energy which creates all forms of existence. This essential energy is vibrating at different frequencies and hence creates the different forms of matter, from fine to dense.

We are so privileged to be living in such exciting times, with modern physics confirming what ancient spiritual and mystical traditions have always taught: *our physical universe is not made of matter but is made of energy. All forms of energy are interrelated and have an effect on each other.* I have written more about this subject in my book *Just Do It Now,* but here we are moving on to consider the implications of these findings on our levels of self-esteem, happiness and success. Because everything is connected it means that the ways we think, feel and act will have a direct influence on others. Of course this also means that we are affected by the thoughts, feelings and behaviour of those around us.

How You Create Your Experiences

People and events really do walk through the doors of your expectations. I know this sounds a bit far-fetched but let's go back to the fundamental truth that the universe is pure energy. Arising from this are The Four Creative Principles, *see* figure 12 (adapted from my book *Just Do It Now*).

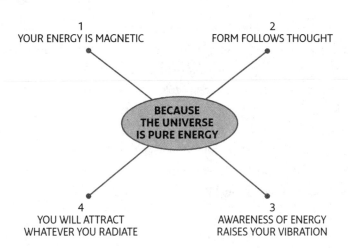

Figure 12: The Four Creative Principles

Because Your Energy is Magnetic You Have Attractive Powers

As atoms are energy fields with positive, negative and neutral charges, they produce electrical and magnetic forces. Electricity attracts, makes you magnetic and draws things to you. The question is, exactly what are you drawing into your life right now? Just as fish swim unconsciously in the water of a tank, so do we swim unconsciously in our universal sea of electromagnetism; every one of our thoughts, feelings and actions registering in this sensitive and delicate 'sea' which surrounds us. The laws governing attracting and repelling operate electromagnetically, which means that energy of a certain quality or vibration tends to attract energy of a similar type and vibration. Think about your 'hunches' and 'gut feelings' that have turned out to be right, and those amazing 'synchronistic' moments that have occurred in your life; these are examples of this principle in action.

Psychologist Carl Jung said that, 'Synchronicity suggests that there is an interconnection or unity of causally unrelated events.' The more you can recognize and respond to the power of your personal magnetism the more powerful it will become! As soon as you connect with the bigger picture of your life, trusting your insights, your intuition and your emotional responses, you will begin to see the way that things so often just naturally click into place. The more you look for meaning and purpose the more of it you will find.

Those who are waiting for the energy they need to get going will be slow to start, whereas those who know that the energy they need is inside them, will find it easy to get into the creative flow of their lives.

EXERCISE

Are You Using Your Intuition?

Sit quietly in a comfortable position and take some deep breaths. Relax your body and your mind. Focus on your intuition.

1 What feelings do you associate with your intuition?

....

....

2 Are these feelings welcome or fearful (or anything else)?

....

....

3 Think of three times that you have followed your intuition and things turned out well.

. . . .

. . . .

. . . .

4 Write down three things that your intuitive voice has been urging you to do. These might only be small things (send that email, read that book) or they may be about bigger issues (change job, end that relationship).

. . . .

. . . .

. . . .

5 Why have you not acted on the advice of your intuition?

. . . .

. . . .

. . . .

Most of us have not been actively encouraged to follow our instincts; it is more likely that we have been taught to reason things out. But of course we need both qualities if our lives are to be a balanced and harmonious experience. Your intuitive voice comes from a place of inner wisdom and the more you become aware of it and act upon it the more powerful it becomes (you enhance your positively magnetic powers).

Intuition speaks to you through feelings, insights, urges, dreams; it is the 'knowing' voice of your spiritual and emotional energy and it will

CONFIDENCE TIP
Develop Your Intuitive Powers

Scientific research demonstrates that a gut reaction is a physical as well as an emotional response. There is a large knot of nerve cells in our stomachs that can respond to any emotional condition and affect our unconscious decisions. Later, when these decisions become conscious, we may become aware that this is something we 'knew' about all along. As we have seen, the more we practise using our intuitive powers the stronger and more reliable they become.

Try the following:

- Take your intuition seriously. Give it the respect it deserves and make time every day to listen in to your inner voice. Find a quiet spot, relax and let your mind rest. Thoughts will come and go but just keep coming back to following your breathing. In this relaxed state you are more aware of your inner world.

always draw you to experiences and people that will energize you and feed your creativity. What sort of future would you like for yourself? Is there something entirely different that you would love to do? You might have a great desire to alter your life in some way but you keep creating excuses, which stop you putting your plans into action. Maybe you are afraid to follow your intuition because it involves change and a degree of risk-taking. But your self-esteem, happiness and success rely on both your self-awareness and your ability to activate your desires, and so it is vital that you follow through for yourself. Your feelings express

- Bring a situation to mind and ask your intuition for guidance. You might get an immediate response but most likely the answer will come later when you are doing something else. Don't expect anything, but know that you have expressed a strong intention here and you have sown a seed that will develop and grow.

- Begin to notice your natural instinctive responses in your day-to-day life. For example when you 'pick up' on someone's mood and 'know' that this would be a bad time to ask for a favour. Or maybe what you thought of as a 'coincidence' begins to take on more meaning and you see a message there. Your inner voice is only really an extension of your everyday awareness, so practise being intuitive.

- When a difficult situation arises and you don't know what to do, turn inside to check your instinctive response: ask yourself what 'feels' right here? If there is no reply then that in itself is a message not to react, and to bide your time.

If you make good friends with your intuition you will have a strong, reliable (inner) partner for life.

your deepest needs and your intuition prompts you to respond to these needs. Ignore your intuition at your peril!

Form Follows Thought so Your Focus Becomes Your Reality

Thoughts are creatively energetic. If we continually focus on something we begin to draw the energy out from our inner world of thoughts and senses to create something in the outer world of reality. Everything starts with a thought: your lunch, the chair you are sitting in, the house you live in, your conception, the internet, your mobile phone, the Sunday papers ... Everything is energy and this energy manifests in different forms to create everything within the universe.

Mind energy (thought) is changeable, quick and has a high vibration (happens instantaneously) – we can experience 50,000 thoughts a day, which just shows how quickly they come and go. Matter is denser energy, more compact and slower to move and change. So you can have the thought *I want a fabulous pair of Jimmy Choo shoes*, but you can't manifest them as quickly as you can think about them (shame!). You can't stand in front of the previously mentioned footwear, stir up your electromagnetic powers and draw them into your life and on to your feet; the process takes a bit longer. Consider the following options:

1 I keep wishing for a pair of Jimmy Choo shoes.
2 I am constantly thinking about what it would be like to wear a pair of his shoes.
3 Each time I look at my shoe rack I see a fabulous pair of red shoes and I am beginning to feel that they are already mine.
4 I visit the Jimmy Choo shop in Knightsbridge and fall in love with a pair of red peep-toe slingbacks. I try them on and walk around the shop in them; they are gorgeous.
5 I take a realistic look at my finances and work out that I can buy them in two months. They can be mine in two months.

If I just stick with wishing for these shoes they will remain a fantasy. But constantly thinking about them focuses my thoughts in their direction and then the strong idea creates a picture; I start to actively visualize them. By now my commitment has definitely intensified and I am off to the shop; I come away knowing they will be mine. I want them so much that I manage my finances so that I can afford them in two months – result unquestionable! My idea is a blueprint that creates an image. The image then magnetizes and directs the physical energy so that it flows into its form and eventually materializes in physical reality.

We know that it is fairly easy to imagine creating simple things: make marmite on toast, drive to the shops, meet up with a friend, buy a birthday present for someone, cycle to work ... These are all creative acts; you have been automatically manifesting things all your life using this simple magnetizing process. Start to become aware of the creative process:

Step 1 You want something.
Step 2 You intend to have it.
Step 3 You are motivated to do what it takes to get it.

You use exactly the same process when you want to make anything happen. Your idea to have something sets up the model of what you will be creating. And then, the strength of your emotions (intention, desire, and motivation) energizes your thoughts and projects them from your inner world into your outer world.

THOUGHT ENERGY	X	EMOTIONAL ENERGY	→	MATERIAL ENERGY

QUICK QUIZ

How Positive Are You Feeling Right Now?

	Yes | No
I feel like smiling	|
I am worrying about the future	|
I like myself	|
I have some regrets and can't let go of them	|
I would like to feel more relaxed	|
I am comparing myself with someone else	|
I wonder if I will ever be happy	|
I know how to increase my positive status	|
I am feeling self-critical	|
I am high in 'can do' energy	|

Notice how the nature of your self-expression has an immediate effect on raising or lowering your energy. Turn the energy-depleting activities around; just stop doing them. Turn up the positive dial immediately and see how this affects you. You take yourself wherever you go and this means *all* of you: your thoughts, emotions, expectations, insights, hang-ups ... etc. At some level, others pick up and respond to the totality of your energetic expression, so embrace and express your magnificent self and wait for the reaction.

You Attract Whatever You Radiate so Make Sure You Radiate Positivity

Think of your magnetic field as an expression of your aliveness, enthusiasm and energy levels. How buzzing are you right now? If you are feeling less than your best, you can consciously raise your spirits by involving yourself in more energy-enhancing activities and by dropping any energy-depleting habits. Check out your radiating status at this very moment. (*See* Quick Quiz on page 184.)

10 Ways to upgrade your vibrations immediately

1   Turn up the music and DANCE!
2   Smile (fake it until you can make it).
3   Contact a positive friend.
4   Go for a walk.
5   Feel glad to be alive (after all, it is pretty amazing).
6   Give something to someone.
7   Go outside and take some deep breaths.
8   Imagine turning up your positive energy dial to the max.
9   Connect with a stranger.
10 Perform an anonymous act of kindness.

Your Awareness of Energy Raises Your Vibration, so Become More Conscious of Your Responses

Novelist Paulo Coelho is an illuminating writer who can open our eyes with his wonderful words. He says: 'You can become blind by seeing each day as a similar one. Each day is a different one, each day brings a miracle of its own. It's just a matter of paying attention to this miracle.' And so our level of awareness depends upon our level of attention.

Imagine this: You drive to town and as you get to the multi-storey car park you suddenly 'come to' and realize that you have driven all this way on autopilot; you can't remember anything about the journey but here you are. You get out of the car to buy a ticket and feel alienated by your concrete surroundings, you don't like it in here and you feel your energy dropping. When you leave the car park you enter a busy shopping mall; everyone is rushing around and it all feels too frenetic so you make for the coffee shop. The woman behind the counter greets you with a big smile and up goes your energy; ah yes, you are feeling much better now. And then a friend calls your mobile and you catch up with your news. Feeling even better you go out and face the mall and now find that you are in the mood to shop.

Observe the thread of awareness running through your experience. On the drive you were totally disengaged, and then gradually became aware as your mood dipped and then rose again. Start to tune into these daily troughs and peaks, in a non-judgemental way, just be interested in how you respond. By bringing increased awareness to your 'low' energy you will notice that your experience will change without you having to do much more. And as you become more aware of your 'uplifted' energy you will recognize that this energy has a certain emotional tone (a high vibration) that you can start to 'tap into' at will. Everything and everybody is connected and we know that this one world has two aspects: the visible and the invisible. This means that by appreciating and understanding the subtle and 'invisible' levels of energy we can change the reality that we can see.

Consider this: *You might not be reaching your goals because you actually fear success.*

Case Study

Rose, 50, is a librarian and I met her at a workshop I was running called 'Attracting Success'. I love the amazing energy that a group can develop, and the way that participants get so much from listening to other people; we all share the trials and tribulations of life, and remembering this can be very healing.

EXERCISE

Honing the Art of Appreciation

Although I have talked about appreciation before, we are now going to dig even deeper to find its true value for us.

When we can feel admiration, gratitude, enjoyment and a sense of wonder, then we are really experiencing the power of appreciation. True appreciation demands that we look, and then look again with the eyes of our senses. Try practising this today. There are many levels of appreciation, going from the most superficial to an in-depth connection; be aware of the ways that you appreciate today. Try:

- being more appreciative by looking for things, people and events to admire and enjoy
- noticing how superficial appreciation feels
- going deeper and look again with the eyes of your senses

There is no right way to do this; see it as an experimental approach to opening your heart to ever deepening levels of appreciation and wonder. Appreciation is a key to increased awareness and we know how awareness can change our inner energy and hence our outer reality – worth a try then!

Someone in the group began to talk about what he saw as the 'pressure of success', which he explained as his anxiety around the thought that once he had achieved a goal he would then be expected to keep up that level of attainment. Others discussed the idea that high self-expectations can lead to disappointment and despair rather than to achievement and success. This naturally led into a discussion about such things as: being good enough, perfectionism and the potential punishing behaviour of our inner critic. The workshop then moved into a stage where participants considered their own glass ceilings (self-imposed limits) and looked for patterns of belief that might be inhibiting them.

After this workshop, Rose had some coaching sessions with me and we talked about some of the things that had come up for her in the group work. She said: 'All the talk of "goal-getting" and "reaching for your dreams" has always had a negative effect on me, making me feel hopeless and low when I know that we need to expect the best in

INSIGHT
Eliminate All Energy-Draining Activities

Because our energy field is magnetic, it is important to be vigilant about any potential energy-draining habits. It is only too easy to find ourselves immersed in negativity and not know how we even got there. Check out the following list to find out exactly what might be depleting your own personal magnetic field.

Are you:

Blaming others - This is an early warning sign of approaching self-pity. As soon as you find yourself scanning the horizon for something or someone to blame, just stop there and notice what you are doing. We all indulge ourselves in the 'blame game' at times so don't criticize yourself for this, just notice it and remember that every time you do this you are giving your own creative power away to your 'victimizer'. Blaming energy is unattractive and always leads to all-lose scenarios.

order for it to happen. So I get in a terrible muddle with all this. In a small group at the workshop I realized how hard I am on myself and I also noticed that I am very judgemental of others when they make a mistake.'

Two weeks later Rose said that she had had a dream where her father was a small boy and she (as an adult) was hitting him with a stick so that he wept for her to stop. Her father had been dead for over 20 years and she said that she had 'locked him away in her mind' until

Feeling regretful – If you made a mistake then all you can do now is to learn from it and move on. Make amends if you can (now) and if you can't, just go swiftly to the present moment, which is where your powerful energy lies.

Wishing you were like someone else – Each time you do this you deny your own unique place in the world. Next time you find yourself making unfavourable comparisons with others become aware of it and make this affirmation: *I am OK just the way I am.* Keep practising and you will break this harmful habit.

Being judgemental – Another early sign of trouble for your confident self! Whoever you are judging, whether it is self or others, this is bad news because it will always diminish you. You will never be at your best if you are looking for the worst in yourself or others.

Stop all energy-drainers and feel your electromagnetic field lighten, brighten and shine. Tune into your personal energy field and sense the positively buzzing vibrations. You take your vibrations wherever you go, so let them be good.

now. Over the next few weeks Rose unlocked a lot of anger and frustration over her relationship with her father. He had been a military man and ran his house in the same fashion. Rose said that she spent her whole childhood trying to please him (an impossible task) and that she couldn't remember one single time when he had praised her.

After a number of sessions Rose began to be able to 'let go' of some of her anger and she saw that her own inner critic had completely taken over from where her father had left off. There is more inner work for her to do, but, as she says, her feelings are now 'out in the open' and she is confident that with continued self-awareness and kindness to herself and to others she can heal her own wounds and open up to some happiness and success in her life.

Don't let your inner critic destroy your confidence. Recognize that constant self-criticism will undermine your self-belief.

Day 8 | Review

Key Reflections for Day 8

- Our physical universe is not made of matter but is made of energy. All forms of energy are interrelated and have an effect on each other.
- People and events walk through the doors of our expectations.
- The more you can recognize and respond to the power of your personal magnetism the more powerful it will become.
- Your feelings express your deepest needs and your intuition prompts you to respond to these needs.
- The more you practise using your intuitive power, the stronger and more reliable it becomes.
- Thoughts are creatively energetic.
- If you are feeling less than your best, you can consciously raise your spirits by involving yourself in more energy-enhancing activities and by dropping any energy-depleting habits.
- Others pick up and respond to the totality of your energetic expression, so embrace and express your magnificent self and just watch the reaction.
- By appreciating and understanding the subtle and 'invisible' levels of energy you can change the reality you see.
- You might not be reaching your goals because you actually fear success.
- Tune into your personal energy field and sense the positively buzzing vibrations: you take your vibrations wherever you go so let them be good.

Your 3-Point Action Plan for Day 8

1 Take any insight that you have made today:
   Example: *When I think about how we are all energetically connected I wonder why I surround myself with people who are quite negative.*

2 Consider the patterns (thought/emotional/behavioural) that might lie behind this:
   Example: *I am very sensitive to other people's energy and often they tell me their problems; I feel I have to listen to them, even if I don't want to.*

3 Create an action point around a possible change of response:
   Example: *I think I need to protect myself from the negative vibrations of other people. I am going to stop being so available to listen to the moans and complaints of others, and even walk away if necessary.*

Try this 3-point action plan for yourself.

My personal insights:

. . . .

. . . .

. . . .

The patterns that might lie behind this:

· ·

· ·

· ·

My action points:

· ·

· ·

· ·

Day 9

Have Brilliant Relationships

Sometimes it's hard to be assertive when we're wired to want love and to please.

Nikki Gemmell (journalist and author)

*My true relationship is my relationship with myself –
all others are simply mirrors of it.*

Shakti Gawain (author)

How many times have you wished that someone would just change the way they were behaving? If only: your boss was more empathetic; your mother less patronizing; your friends less demanding; your partner more understanding ... (consider your own examples here) how marvellous your life would be! Fill in the following table.

The Ways I Would Like People To Change

Name .... *I would like this person to be ...*

....

Name .... *I would like this person to be ...*

....

Name .... *I would like this person to be ...*

....

Or perhaps you have wished for the perfect man or woman to enter your orbit (and who hasn't done this?). But notice how these projected desires merely return us to the role of dependent victim; waiting and hoping for someone to be different, waiting and wishing to meet the man or woman of our dreams.

Seven Relationship Realities

When I wrote my book *Weekend Love Coach*, I spent some time researching old and new ideas around relationship theory; I also ran an online questionnaire and spoke to many people to hear their own experiences and thoughts. These investigations led me to a number of very interesting conclusions:

1 It is impossible to change another person.
2 We can only change the nature of a relationship by changing ourselves.
3 We might feel unable to leave a poor relationship even when we know that it is not good for us.
4 When we appreciate ourselves we become love magnets, and when we don't we become victims of love.
5 When we are true to ourselves we can make good relationship choices.
6 Sometimes the best we can do is to just walk away.
7 When our personal boundaries are strong we will have healthy relationships.

Changing Another, Changing Yourself

Women are especially keen on the idea of changing others, and we try to do this right across the board, saving our very best efforts for changing the men in our lives! Jerry Hall spent 25 years patiently waiting for Mick (Jagger) to stop his philandering ways. She says: 'I really did think that I could change him. I thought he would settle down and be a wonderful partner, father and husband.' However, in the end, even she had to give up. Nearly all women allow themselves to be seduced by the myth that they, and they alone, have the power to change the things they don't like about their partner. But if we don't step free of this 'neediness' we will remain trapped in the negative spiral of ever falling self-esteem.

Look back at the list of those you would like to change and the ways you would like them to be different. How can you alter these people? Have you ever successfully transformed anyone? The truth is that you cannot change anybody and the more you try to do so the worse the situation will get. Whenever you are waiting for someone to change you are acting like a victim; giving away your power to the other person. If your happiness ever depends upon the actions of others then you have lost control of your life and you will feel low in self-respect, disempowered and angry! Reflect on the last time you found yourself giving your power away; what were the consequences of you doing this?

Next time you notice yourself waiting and hoping for anyone to change, stop immediately and consider this wonderful liberating truth:

The ways that people treat me are reflections of the ways I treat myself.

In other words, the types of relationships that you attract depend entirely on the quality of your own thoughts, feelings, beliefs and expectations. If you are high in self-respect then others will respond well and treat you with the respect that you deserve. If you love and appreciate yourself then you will draw out those qualities in others (remember how we attract what we radiate?). Similarly, if you treat yourself badly, then others will be sure to do the same. If you victimize yourself you will certainly attract the sort of person who is looking for a victim, and if you are low in self-esteem it won't take much to convince everyone that you are not worth valuing. And if you blame yourself, well you can be sure that very soon you will be everybody's scapegoat.

Relationships are made within us but this may be difficult to remember, particularly when we need the approval of others. We have been brought up on a diet of romantic fiction and similar mind-bending entertainments that have taught us to look outside ourselves for our happiness, wellbeing and fulfilment. Our search for Prince/Princess Charming will never be successful; we will always be disappointed. Just as I am writing this I can catch the strains of Marvin Gaye in the background singing: 'Too busy thinkin' 'bout my baby. Ain't got time for nothing else.' Not such a good omen for a relationship but an example of the popular view of romance. Start listening closely to the words of songs and notice where the focus lies.

When we change our focus there may be an initial sense of loss – a loss of potential excitement/danger/the unknown. Why are we so attracted to giving our power away? Perhaps because we really feel we want someone to take good care of us. The pattern of our present relationships is closely linked with the relationship we had with our parents. As babies we are very sensitive to the emotional vibrations around us and as soon as we become aware of our parents' emotional pain, we try to make it right for them; to keep them happy so that they carry on looking after us. This feels like a survival issue to the tiny, vulnerable and needy baby, and so, pleasing its parents becomes vitally important. Our future relationships will tend towards this underlying emotional pattern, which expresses itself like this:

*I will try to be what you want me to be if you will stay
with me and give me what I need.*

Do you recognize this theme in any of your relationships? If you do then I am sure that you know this way of running relationships just doesn't work. People can't always be what we want them to be and so we inevitably feel let down. We might then try to change them or we may give up, submit and become resentful, or we may leave and look for someone else who we think will give us what we need.

EXERCISE

Checking Out Your Relationship Behaviour

(a) Changing another person

Think of a time when you tried to change someone; this can be anyone that you are/were having a relationship with (friend, family member, partner).

Be specific about the changes you were seeking.

The behaviour I wanted to change was:

. . . .

. . . .

What exactly did you do to bring about these changes?

I tried to change this behaviour by:

. . . .

. . . .

Reflect on what happened when you did this.

The outcome of the situation was:

. . . .

Can you describe the type of relationship you now have with this
person?

Our relationship now is:

. . . .

. . . .

Did your attempts to alter this person have any effect on your
relationship? If so, what happened?

Our relationship changed in the following ways:

. . . .

. . . .

It is only possible to make changes in a relationship if you yourself are
prepared to change. All the time you are focusing on the other person
is time wasted looking in the wrong direction.

(b) Choosing to stay in a poor relationship

Have you ever stayed in an unhappy relationship? If so, can you
describe it?

This relationship is/was unsatisfactory because:

. . . .

. . . .

I tried to change this relationship.   yes | no

I chose to stay in this relationship because:

....

....

I would describe my feelings for the other person as:

....

....

I am still in this relationship.   yes | no

My feelings about myself are:

....

....

I would describe myself as having high/low self-esteem.

....

CONFIDENCE TIP

Glow With Social Confidence

How come some people can charm the birds out of the trees while others can only be described as shrinking violets? How about you? Are you always in the kitchen at parties? Would you like to know how to tap into some social confidence skills and feel more at ease with people? Try the following:

Get over yourself and get going. Life is too short to waste time in endless navel-gazing. If you want a vibrant social life then you have to put in the effort and get out there and take a chance. You have nothing to lose except loneliness.

Adopt a more flexible attitude. If you are inclined to stick to the same 'type' of friends and lovers you might have become socially limited because of this. Open your mind to new and interesting people; spread your net wider and give everyone a chance to shine.

Let others inspire you. As soon as you appreciate the good in others they will begin to naturally respond to you. We all warm towards people who encourage our self-belief and show us respect.

If you have tried unsuccessfully to change the nature of a relationship and you still find yourself involved, then look closely at your motives. Are you living out the underlying 'pleasing' theme that you developed with your parents when you were a baby? Do you need to please people; do you need to be 'looked after' at any cost?

There is a double irony in this situation. First, we can hardly feel 'looked after' in an unhappy relationship, and second, what we

Choose the shyest person in the room and get them talking. Four great results here: (1) you realize that you are not the only shrinking violet; (2) you help them to relax; (3) you *appear* outgoing and confident; (4) you *feel* outgoing and confident!

Develop your listening skills. Listening is surely the most underrated communication skill and also must be the easiest. All you have to do is listen! Ask an open question (one which needs a few words to answer) and then focus attentively on the other person. Before you know it you will have a conversation going.

Demonstrate your interest in others by using positive body language. Make good eye-contact and adopt a relaxed posture; immediately the other person will feel at ease.

Take the pressure off by keeping the atmosphere light and positive. People love to laugh, so give them a reason to; don't be afraid to have fun!

Fall in love with your life and you will become an irresistible love magnet. Try this now!

are most looking for *outside* ourselves is the caring, nurturing and approving that only we can provide for ourselves. Are you wired to please or can you dare to please yourself? We are no longer babies; we can take responsibility for our own care (physically and emotionally), we are free to be our naturally confident selves.

10 ways to please yourself

1 Stop doing things that you don't want to do.
2 Say what you mean, not what you think others want you to say.
3 Respect yourself as well as respecting others.
4 Act assertively.
5 Communicate clearly.
6 Tap into your creativity and natural positivity.
7 Take time out to 'be' rather than to 'do'.
8 Trust your gut instincts and act accordingly.
9 Remember that you too deserve to be happy.
10 Befriend yourself; this relationship is for life!

How to be a Love Magnet

When we can love and appreciate ourselves we will attract loving and appreciative relationships. This is easy to go along with when our relationships are blooming, but when we are feeling badly used it can be hard to believe. Relationship experts Marni Kamins and Janice Macleod remind us that: 'While you are in a relationship, it can sometimes feel as if the goal is to love your man as best you can so that he will be happy, and thus you will be happy. However, the true goal is to love yourself in good times and bad, no matter what.'

Ah, good times *and bad*, now that is a big ask! First let me tell you a secret: even life coaches get grumpy! Yes it's quite true. And fabulous go-getting self-believers; charismatic alluring love magnets; assertive, trailblazing winners – they all have their days off! No one is confident all the time so just let yourself off this particular aspirational hook right now and things will get a whole lot easier. I know that in life coaching we say things like, 'expect the best' and 'you get what you think you deserve', and for sure it is important to stretch ourselves beyond our limiting self-beliefs, but it is only too easy to turn our personal development journey into a massive test where yet again we are never 'good enough'. Appreciating and valuing yourself does not mean loving only your positive, confident, sociable, brilliant and intelligent selves; it means loving your whole self; and this means warts and all! The real challenge comes in loving your disbelieving, self-doubting, fed-up, grumpy and judgemental selves.

When you can accept your own human moodiness then you will be less self-critical and this leads to increased self-esteem and happiness, which leads to relaxed and improved relationships with others.

SELF-   →   INCREASED   →   IMPROVED
ACCEPTANCE   SELF-ESTEEM   RELATIONSHIPS

Think of, say, a woman you know who is confident and sociable and consider her talents. She might not be the best-looking woman in the room but she will have a certain inner style that draws others to her like a magnet. She attracts the attention of others (both men and women) because she radiates certain qualities. Take a look at the following diagram.

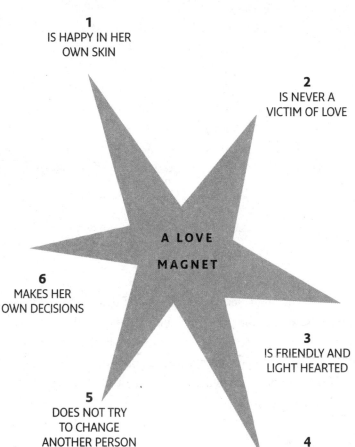

1
IS HAPPY IN HER
OWN SKIN

2
IS NEVER A
VICTIM OF LOVE

A LOVE

MAGNET

6
MAKES HER
OWN DECISIONS

3
IS FRIENDLY AND
LIGHT HEARTED

5
DOES NOT TRY
TO CHANGE
ANOTHER PERSON

4
BELIEVES THAT
SHE DESERVES
GREAT RELATIONSHIPS

Figure 13: The Qualities of a Love Magnet

QUICK QUIZ

Are You Magnetizing Love Right Now?

Reflect upon each of the six qualities. Would you say that these statements are true or untrue for you?

Score 2 each time you answer – True
Score 0 each time you answer – Untrue

If you scored 10-12

Things are looking very good for you. Even if you are not in a significant relationship at the moment, you have the inner confidence and belief to attract positive people into your life. Keep radiating those good vibrations and just you wait and see who walks through the doors of your expectations!

If you scored 6-8

You have what it takes to be a love magnet. Even if only three of these qualities are true for you, this demonstrates a certain degree of 'attracting' power. Look at where you scored 0 and raise your game in these areas. What would you need to believe about yourself to obtain the maximum score? Begin to believe it!

If you scored 2-4

Review the quality (or qualities) that were true for you. Imagine that you are demonstrating this quality now and really get into this feeling of optimism and confidence. Now all you need to do is to demonstrate *more* of this assertiveness; carry this positive energy into every area of your life and you will be amazed by who you will attract.

If you scored 0

Your positively 'attracting' qualities will kick in as soon as you decide that enough self-criticism is enough! Keep working on the techniques in this book and remember that you deserve to be happy and that you are ready to take the next exciting step on your journey. Start by repeating this mantra: *I am a love magnet.* You see, it works; you are smiling already.

Finding the Balance

Your partner wants to do this, you want to do that. A friend wants you to babysit but you have already made plans. Your child wants you to be a taxi service and you want an early night. A colleague needs you to stay late to help finish an important piece of work and you have a hot date. So many times we are faced with this dilemma – how do we find the balance between being a: loving partner/parent /child; good friend; supportive colleague; and also taking care of our own needs?

In psychology we speak of healthy and unhealthy relationships, and you can very easily work out which category each of your relationships falls into. A healthy relationship is one where you are able to satisfy your own basic needs, and you can identify these needs by becoming aware of your personal boundaries.

Counsellor Robert Burney explains what it means to set up personal boundaries: 'The purpose of having boundaries is to protect and take care of ourselves. We need to be able to tell other people when they are acting in ways that are not acceptable to us. A first step is starting to know that we have a right to protect and defend ourselves. That we have not only the right, but the duty to take responsibility for how we allow others to treat us.'

Think of a time when somebody invaded your physical boundaries and your reaction to that. Now consider a more subtle level of invasion, at the emotional level – when did this last happen to you and how did you feel? You will quickly know when your emotional boundaries are being invaded; someone will be too familiar or push you too far and you will immediately feel uncomfortable. As soon as this happens, check your boundaries. You do this by asking yourself: 'How far am I prepared to go with this person?'

Naturally you will set different boundaries in each of your relationships; for example you might tell your best friend something that you would not share with your partner. Perhaps your ability to trust others will set different limits on your willingness to open up. And of course your boundaries are flexible and will change (as you grow more or less intimate with others). You can always judge the health of a particular relationship by understanding it in terms of how far you can go with anyone (physically or emotionally) *and still feel comfortable.* If you are ever uncomfortable in a relationship, you have allowed yourself to go beyond your personal boundaries and you need to stop and re-evaluate what you are allowing to happen and why.

Wherever you have a boundary problem you will also have low self-esteem. Poor relationships, unhealthy boundaries and low self-esteem go hand in hand.

Consider this: *Low self-confidence leads to unhealthy boundaries which always lead to poor relationships.*

INSIGHT

Maintaining Healthy Boundaries

You are in control of all your relationships and it is good to remember this when things get tricky. Because we teach others how to treat us, it is possible to change ourselves and so change our relationships. Whether you are considering your family, friendships or love life, you can always draw a new line in the sand, which effectively says: you can go this far and no further. Your new expectations and behaviour will certainly alter any relationship dynamic; the other person might rise to the occasion and be prepared to change their ways or this might mean the end of your relationship. Sometimes we do outgrow people and situations and then all we can do is let go and move on.

How to draw a new line in the sand

Reflect on any relationship difficulty that you have at the moment and try this activity:

Case Study

Sarita, 34, a senior project manager in the healthcare sector rang me in despair. Tom, her boyfriend of four years had ended their relationship a few months ago and she described herself as having absolutely zero self-esteem and not knowing which way to turn. I think of the end of a relationship as a type of bereavement, and it can take any amount of recovery time. But by the time Sarita and I talked she had been crying in her cocoa for long enough and was now feeling pretty angry with Tom and with herself.

- Be specific about what is happening.

Example – My partner doesn't get on well with my grown-up children and I feel divided loyalty.

- Is there anything you can do about this?

Example – I can speak to them all and tell them how uncomfortable I feel.

- How did this work out?

Example – My children were a bit embarrassed but my partner said that he understood.

- What action did you take to improve the situation?

Example – We decided to invite the children and their partners around for a family social evening.

- How did this work?

Example – It was excellent, everyone made an effort and I felt much more relaxed about everything.

She described her relationship history as being very poor: 'I am just so bad at keeping blokes and I have only ever lived with Tom. I had hoped that this was going to last but he has always been a bit temperamental and I was forever thinking, is he going to stay or go? Last year he went skiing with his mates and I discovered that he had a fling with a girl while he was out there. He brushed it off and I decided to just forget about it – he has had a few flings over the time we have been together so I didn't take it too seriously. But then he met someone at work and said that he couldn't be what I wanted him to be and that I was just too needy and it made him feel claustrophobic. I was so hurt at first and I could hardly get out of bed but thankfully my great job saved me from total hibernation.'

I asked Sarita to tell me a bit more about Tom's 'flings' and she said that she had got used to him 'going off' occasionally but always expected him to come back. I asked her how she had felt when he saw other women and she said that she was humiliated but 'always just hoped he'd come back to her'. When I suggested that she had allowed Tom to behave badly she found it hard to see how this could be. But over the course of a few weeks she became more in touch with her deeper emotions and started to recognize her own unhealthy boundaries. We did some work on building her self-confidence and she began to socialize again. A few months later she contacted me to say that she was feeling much better and that she had met someone who treated her well and helped her to feel positive about herself, and then she said, 'I can't believe what I let Tom get away with, I must have felt so low about myself.'

Working on creating healthy boundaries is a wonderfully practical and direct way to increase your self-esteem.

Day 9 | Review

Key Reflections for Day 9

- Your most important relationship will always be the one that you have with yourself.
- We cannot change another person however patiently we wait.
- Remember that you, too, deserve to be happy.
- As soon as you begin to appreciate the good in others they will naturally begin to respond to you.
- Believe that you deserve brilliant relationships and you will begin to attract them.
- When you are true to yourself you make good relationship choices.
- Fall in love with your life and you will become an irresistible love magnet.
- We are responsible for the ways that we let others treat us.
- Create healthy boundaries and your self-esteem will automatically rise.
- Sometimes we outgrow people and situations and then all we can do is let go and move on.

Your 3-Point Action Plan for Day 9

1 Take any insight that you have made today:
   Example: *I never feel totally myself when I am in a relationship, and if my partner is angry I always assume that it is my fault.*

2 Consider the patterns (thought/emotional/behavioural) that might lie behind this:
   Example: *I am overanxious to please and this means I often ignore my own feelings.*

3 Create an action point around a possible change of response:
   Example: *I am gradually becoming more aware of when I go into 'pleasing' mode and am already beginning to change this reaction.*

Try this 3-point action plan for yourself.

My personal insights

. . . .

. . . .

. . . .

The patterns that might lie behind this

. . . .

. . . .

....

....

My action points

....

....

....

....

Day 10

Maintain Your High Self-Esteem

Always be a first-rate version of yourself, instead of a second-rate version of somebody else.

Judy Garland (actress and singer)

'Now I'll give you something to believe. I'm just one hundred and one, five months and a day.'

*'I can't believe **that**!' said Alice.*

'Can't you?' the Queen said in a pitying tone. 'Try again: draw a long breath, and shut your eyes.'

*Alice laughed. 'There's no use trying,' she said: 'One **can't** believe in impossible things.'*

'I daresay you haven't had much practice,' said the Queen. 'When I was your age, I always did it for half an hour a day. Why sometimes I've believed as many as six impossible things before breakfast.'

Lewis Carroll, *Alice Through the Looking Glass*

Your self-esteem is built upon your self-belief, and throughout this book we have been developing techniques to increase our belief in ourselves. I know that sometimes it must have felt as though I was asking you to believe in 'impossible' things. When we are feeling very low it is hard to remember that we are special, worthy and lovable. But it is constantly true. *You are always special, worthy and lovable.* It is at these times, when the going is hard, that we most need to believe in ourselves. Belief is strong magic.

On each day of this programme you have used many different methods to help you feel more confident and self-assured, but at the root of each of these techniques is one simple message: *Learn to love yourself.* And if this sometimes feels like an 'impossible' task then *practise* it. Practise believing that you are wonderful, amazing, deserving, significant – because you are.

Create your own list of affirming self-beliefs. Keep these affirmations in the present tense; keep them positive and keep saying them, *all the time.* Refer to this list immediately you feel your self-esteem falling. Use these examples if you wish and create some more of your own.

Examples

I love and value myself

I am a wonderful and creative person

I deserve the best in life

My list of positive affirmations

. . . .

. . . .

. . . .

I have successfully used all the techniques and ideas that I write about, and I began my own personal development journey by using affirmations. Sometimes they get a bad press. Well, it is certainly true that occasionally remembering to say, 'I love myself' is not going to have a dramatic effect on your personal development, but the *concentrated application* of affirmations will lead to an influx of new energy as you contradict old negative patterns and replace outmoded and useless negative beliefs. The CBT domino effect then kicks in:

fresh positive → new upbeat → enlivened and
beliefs   emotions   confident actions

You will only change your habitual negativity if you really become mindful of how you are thinking, what you are thinking, and the language that you use to communicate with others and with yourself. It can be a shock to discover how we drone on in our speech (and in our heads) in such an unhelpful manner: criticizing, judging, complaining ... no wonder we struggle to feel good about ourselves! But once we have realized what we are doing we have access to the most powerful tool – with an ongoing concentrated focus we can begin to like ourselves a bit more and then our lives really do take off.

I have positive affirmations on the wall of my office and, periodically, when I have had time to get too used to them, I take them down and put up some more. I also write useful upbeat statements on small coloured cards and keep them handy for reference. Clients are often surprised that I have these constant reminders around, but we all need them because it is only too easy to get distracted and lost in what we consider to be our inabilities and deficiencies. And this leads on nicely into the topic for today which is the importance of maintaining our self-esteem.

Maintenance Work

You may have read this book and practised the techniques, but you will always need to do your maintenance work. You will *always* be working on your self-esteem because it reflects your own relationship with yourself and this is always changing and developing. Any method which helps you to increase and maintain your levels of self-esteem will be based on the concept of self-nurturing. As soon as we begin to nurture ourselves we sow the seeds of self-esteem. If we feel depressed, unworthy, unlovable, rejected, critical and low in any way, the first steps to recovery always begin with our decision to take care of ourselves; in this way we replace the laser beam of self-discontent with the laser beam of self-respect and self-love.

Here are 10 self-nurturing activities that I think of as a first-aid kit to delve into as soon as we feel a wobble coming on. We have looked at all these techniques in the book and some will have resonated with you more than others. Which ones do you favour and why? Consider the others; there might be something in them for you. Sometimes we stick to the same old things that seem to work, and are averse to trying others that might seem a bit demanding – stretch yourself here, be creatively self-supportive.

Figure 14: Self-Nurturing Activities

Look for the path with a heart: When a challenge arises you can make an immediate decision – to sink or not. Do you let yourself go under and become overwhelmed by negativity and self-doubt, or do you surf those choppy waters? The choice is simple – look for the course of action that inspires you and feels 'right' and 'lifts' your energy.

Use assertion techniques: Get behind yourself wholeheartedly, stand up for what you want and communicate your needs clearly. If you don't want to be treated like a doormat then don't act like one. Think of an assertive act as being an act of kindness, to yourself and to others – when you are being open and honest everyone benefits.

Cultivate kindness to yourself: In Day 1 we considered that lack of kindness to the self is the seed of low self-esteem, and so here is a direct route to increased confidence and happiness. You will know only too well how unkind you can be to poor old you – just stop this behaviour and treat yourself like a loved one. What could you do to show yourself some TLC? – do it!

Stop comparison shopping: Conditioned as we are to achieving, striving and competing, it is hardly surprising that we are habituated to comparing ourselves with others. You will have experienced how feelings of low self-worth can drive you into judging and evaluating your performance in relation to others. Whether you compare upwards (he is so much more talented than me) or downwards (I am so much prettier than her) you are on dangerous ground. Become mindful of your comparison tendencies and remember that they will definitely lead you under the waves!

Use positive language: We magnify the miserable, dissatisfied and 'can't do' mindset whenever we indulge in thoughts and words of a negative nature. Buoyant and upbeat words have amazing spirit-lifting qualities. Whenever your mood dips, use your positive affirmations and check the quality of the thoughts revolving in your head; remember that a PMA (positive mental attitude) will change your reality.

Listen to your intuition: In times of doubt, seek your own opinion; your wise self knows all the best moves you can make – listen to it and act upon it. You can trust your own instincts, and the more you do the stronger you will become.

Express your emotions: Because our feelings are a direct expression of our needs it is vital that we give them the attention they deserve. Sometimes we cover up our feelings and internalize them, and we all know how this leads us to a low and confused place. Check that you have said what you need to say and respect your needs; this will always support your self-respect and self-esteem.

Open your heart to yourself: This is a rather beautiful way to reflect on our spirituality. We operate on so many levels and this can be easy to forget. If we are feeling overwhelmed by our physical presence, our thoughts or our emotions, we can override this negative mood by simply remembering that we are spiritual beings who are desperately trying to be human, and that this is certainly not always easy for us. Take a moment now to drop any physical, mental and emotional pre-occupations and simply step into your spiritual energy. Not sure how to do this?

Try stopping for a moment, take a few conscious breaths, and just imagine opening up your heart. Visualize your heart area surrounded by warm, soft, pink light and then expand the light to envelop your whole body – bathe in your loveliness; now how do you feel?

Be aware of your inner critic: You have been listening to this voice for your whole lifetime and usually only with depressing results!

The concept of self-nurturing is alien to your inner critic whose *raison d'être* is to keep you on the hop: unsure and self-doubting. Nurturing means taking care of yourself; this is recognizing internal put-downs and then deciding to ignore them. When you make a conscious effort to break this unrewarding pattern you will be filled with confidence and self-respect.

Visualize a positive outcome: We know that if we change the thought, we change the emotions and actions related to that thought. But don't forget that 'thoughts' also manifest mentally in picture form (think: dreams, imaginings and fantasies). So you can create a new positive outcome by 'seeing' it in your mind's eye and this then creates matching thoughts; and so the CBT process can be set in motion in this way. If your thoughts and pictures are not matching (e.g. your affirmation is that 'I am a winner' and you are 'seeing' your inevitable failure, then this will sabotage your good result).

The Importance of an Inner and Outer Action Plan

As a Capricorn I have a natural inclination to love planning, but this has not always proved to be a helpful tendency! In the days before I understood the way that the mind helps to create the reality of our experience, I often used half-baked plans to try to manage any situation that was running out of control – work, relationships, health issues, friendships ... but more often than not my plans failed. And this was because action does not just entail going out and making things happen. This of course will be part of the plan, what we might call our *outer plan*, but there must also be an *inner plan* – and the two must be in alignment if we are to succeed in reaching our goal.

We know that outer changes are a reflection of inner changes (we attract what we radiate) and so a goal-getting plan needs to address the

CONFIDENCE TIP

Create an Appreciation List

This is such a good tip to use in an emergency situation when self-doubt kicks in and down you go, catastrophizing all the way. (Catastrophizing means making mountains out of molehills.)

Whenever this starts just make an appreciation list and you will quickly get things back in perspective. Appreciation revives your self-esteem.

Example

I Lynda, appreciate my gorgeous granddaughter.

I Lynda, appreciate the beautiful flowers in my garden.

I Lynda, appreciate the bravery and positivity of my elderly parents.

I .... appreciate ....

I .... appreciate ....

I .... appreciate ....

This is such an uplifting thing to do, why wait until panic sets in?

direction of our energy at all levels – mental, emotional, spiritual and physical. *Thought creates form* is one of the four principles of creativity, and the following expression (which we looked at on page 183), reminds us how the creative process works.

THOUGHT   X   EMOTIONAL   →   MATERIAL
ENERGY   ENERGY   ENERGY

Achieving any goal, whether it's a new pair of shoes or a total change in self-image, depends upon an alchemical process involving belief, vision, commitment and action. Nothing can change for us unless we can imagine that it will; our belief must be total. Our visions (of how the changes will manifest) must support our belief, and then the necessary physical energy will naturally be channelled into creating the new goals.

It is only too easy to forget your sheer brilliance and amazingness! We can all slip into self-doubt at any time and your best defence is to keep reminding yourself that you are special, worthy and lovable.

Check Your Energy at All Levels

Reflect on the contents of your journal. Take a look at your answers to the various exercises, checklists and questions. Notice any patterns that might emerge and review your personal action plans and insights at the end of each chapter. Now see how these findings relate to each 'type' of energy described below.

1 Your mental energy

This is your mind energy; your ideas, thoughts and beliefs, and as you know, all change starts here, with an idea! Where do you need to turn your mind around? What negative affirmations might be holding you back? Take such a statement and contradict it. For example, if you believe that: *nobody cares what I do*, then change this and affirm that, *my contribution is important*. Or if you think that: *I can't trust my decision-making powers*, then change this to *I can trust my own judgement*.

Recognizing your habitual negative thoughts is a very important starting point for effective change, so don't get demoralized by your own mental patterns – see them for what they are and then change them. Some effort is required here; they won't change overnight, but your continuing awareness and application of positive contradicting statements will break up your habitual negative mindsets.

2 Your spiritual energy

Positive affirmations of intent must be supported by accompanying positive visions, or they will not work. And here you direct your spiritual energy, by looking inside yourself and creatively visualizing the realization of your goals. Stop, relax and slow down your breathing. In your mind's eye, see, feel and experience yourself making your dreams come true. For example, if you want to be more successful then see yourself thriving and hear and feel the admiration and acclaim of others. Get really specific and fill in the details of your visualization – exactly how will your success look? Experience this in full Technicolor with the sound turned up! Get right into the skin of your successful self and let your new images replace those old outmoded pictures that didn't work for you.

NEGATIVE AFFIRMATIONS	+	NEGATIVE VISUALIZATIONS	→	OLD NEGATIVE REALITIES
POSITIVE AFFIRMATIONS	+	POSITIVE VISUALIZATIONS	→	NEW CHANGED REALITIES

3 Your emotional energy

The strength of your beliefs and expectations, fired by the power of your imagination, come together and attract your outcomes. Your desire to make changes must be powerful. Check the intensity of your motivation; are you totally inspired by your goal? Are you driven by a burning desire to succeed? If you are still holding back then maybe the time is not quite right for you to act. On the other hand it might be a good idea to dig a little deeper into your emotional energy and consider whether you have any feelings that might be limiting your progress. Look back at your journal entries and reflect on your emotional responses. Are you connected to your feelings, are you able to express them? Or is there a block in your emotional energy?

Work on clarifying your emotions. Start asking yourself at regular intervals throughout the day, 'how am I feeling'? This is a brilliant way to open up to your emotional energy. Confused and unexpressed emotions can ruin the clarity of purpose that you need to become self-motivated.

4 Your physical energy

Action never stands alone! Your new positive affirmations and visualizations, fired by the enthusiasm of total commitment, will naturally produce the right action to create your new outcome. Your behaviour patterns are a reflection of the ways you think and feel about yourself and your world – what are your actions reflecting to you at the moment? If you see yourself as a victim then it will be difficult for you to trust your decision-making processes and to carry things through to a conclusion; something or someone will always stop you from reaching your goal. But when you adopt a creative response to life then your attitude of self-respect and openheartedness allows you to behave assertively and to take full responsibility for your actions.

Notice if there are any areas of your life where you are: afraid to take a risk; reluctant to say no, or anxious about asking for what you want. If there are, then concentrate on being more assertive and improving your communication skills – it is not so much *what* you do that counts but rather, *how* you do it.

From Dream To Reality – A Useful Action Plan

As you move from your intention towards the realization of a goal you might find it helpful to structure your thoughts by using the action plan in the table on pages 230–31 .

Intention: State one of your goals.

I want to
. . . .

. . . .

Method: Decide what steps you will need to take. Try putting them in the order that they need to be dealt with; this might take some consideration.

Needs: List all the resources that you will need. These could include: help, specialist advice, training, finance, premises, coaching, family support … your initial list may change as time passes and conditions change.

Review: Give yourself some realistic deadlines. Decide on certain dates when you will look at your progress and see how you are doing.

Any changes: This is your flexibility column. Your plan needs to have inbuilt flexibility so that you can respond to changes in a creative way instead of being floored if things don't go the way you expected. New entries here may affect the other columns, so be prepared to make continual changes to your written action plan.

Explaining this makes it sound much more complicated than it actually is. Just remember that it is *your* plan and there are no right and wrong ways to go about it. It might be useful to make a copy of it, on paper or on screen, especially if you have a number of objectives. You can use this structure to help you pursue any goals whether they are short-, medium- or long-term. Utilize this plan so that it works for you.

If your goal feels too far-fetched (e.g. 'I want to be a rock star') you could start a little closer to home (and begin with having singing lessons and learning to play the guitar). Everything happens just one simple step at a time – this is how things unfold. You can only take the step which is directly in front of you, and until you have made that move you will not be equipped for the next. If your goal feels very distant, just take the step that you need to take right now. Use your inner and outer action plans and believe in your goal. There is no time to lose – take a leap of faith and follow your star!

From Dream To Reality - A Useful Action Plan

INTENTION – State your goal	METHOD – List the steps you need to take

NEEDS – List the resources you will need	REVIEW – Decide a date to review progress	ANY CHANGES – Note any changes that are needed

INSIGHT

Let Your Regrets Increase Your Awareness

Finding the value in our 'mistakes' is a truly insightful move. Rather than looking back with regret at all those times we wished we had acted in a different way, we can turn these occasions into real opportunities to move on and grow.

- Choose an incident that you regret and ask yourself: what would I have done differently with hindsight? What have I learned from this? Let this vital knowledge inform your future behaviour.

- Notice that many of your regrets revolve around things that you *didn't* do rather than the things you would like to have done differently. We are often most sorry about the opportunities we didn't take. Let this realization be a stark reminder to take your chances when they arise – *carpe diem*!

Consider this: *You might be using powerful visualization techniques and be highly focused and determined, and still feel unable to accomplish your goal*

Case Study

Dawn, 28, was a client of mine who went back to university to gain an MSc in human resource management and had begun working in a university HR department. From day one she struggled with an overload of information and a lack of confidence in managing her workload. After two weeks she rang me in tears to say she couldn't cope and yet she thought that she 'should' be able to. She told me that this was her dream job and that she had visualized and worked hard for this job opportunity, and yet here she was, making 'a complete mess of everything' and each day it was getting harder to go in. Dawn was low in confidence and definitely slipping downwards to the bottom of a negative spiral.

She was surprised to have fallen apart in this way and said: 'Why has this happened to me when I have been so focused and committed and worked so hard for this opportunity? On paper I "should" be sailing through this and making a really good impression but I think my colleagues have a very low opinion of my abilities and this makes me even more likely to make a mistake.'

Goals are demanding; we achieve them and then they stretch us even more to develop and grow. Everything changes and we also need to adapt to new situations. There was no time for Dawn to rest on her laurels; she really needed to galvanize herself pretty quickly to meet the demands of the job. I reminded her that we always have to change and move on, we are a work in progress, and as such she just needed to hold her nerve here and be more self-supporting. She really was giving herself such a hard time and only two weeks into the job! I suggested that she gave herself a break and stopped expecting to be faultless.

In conversation Dawn often used the word 'should', and I challenged her use of this word. When we say that we 'should' be doing something or other we reveal our critical and self-demeaning beliefs. The word 'should' always suggests that we are, or soon will be, wrong in some way. Over the course of a few sessions we worked together on maintaining positive thoughts by not using critical words (such as 'should') and by building up a realistic picture of what she needed to achieve in the workplace and how best to activate this. After our first session Dawn felt more confident and assertive and over the next month began to feel more settled in the job.

We can be so hard on ourselves, even when we are doing well. Sometimes the better we do, the more we expect of ourselves – we need to watch this tendency because it always leads to low self-esteem. When the going gets rough, remember to be kinder to yourself!

Checking Your Levels of Self-Esteem

Scale of feelings

Your self-esteem at its lowest

1 Totally depressed, utterly miserable

2 Unhappy or sad

3 Not satisfied, unfulfilled

4 Sometimes alright, sometimes not

5 Quite satisfied

6 Pleased, positive, very satisfied

7 Delighted, thrilled, very happy

Your self-esteem at its highest

This scale of feelings from 1 to 7 represents the range of emotions from your lowest levels of self-esteem to your highest. Check your self-esteem levels in all areas of your life by filling in the Self-Esteem Progress Chart on page 236. Put a dot in each of the appropriate columns and connect the dots vertically. Use a coloured pencil and make a note of the date you used it in the Colour Key below. When you chart your levels again use another colour and then you can compare your self-esteem levels at different times.

Colour Key

Date   Colour
....

Date   Colour
....

Date   Colour
....

Date   Colour
....

Date   Colour
....

Date   Colour
....

Date   Colour
....

Date   Colour
....

Self-Esteem Progress Chart

	1	2	3	4	5	6	7
Intimate relationship							
Friendships, social life							
Family relationships							
Creative pursuits							
Work, job, main occupation							
General health							
Fitness, physical activities							
Financial situation							
Levels of resistance to victimization							
Freedom of emotional expression							
Ambitions, goals, outcomes							
Trust in own intuition							
Time management							
Levels of self-awareness							
Quantity of 'me' time							
Quality of 'me' time							
Ability to be forgiving							
Enjoyment of sensual pleasures							
Enjoyment of fun activities							
Levels of success, recognition							
Ability to relax and let go							

After you have used the chart a few times you will see the peaks and troughs that occur in the different areas of your life. This chart will help you to see which areas you need to work on. You will then be able to go back into the book and find the specific techniques that you will need to use to increase your self-esteem in these particular areas. And in this way you can develop your own personal self-esteem action plan.

Remember that as you learn to increase your feelings of self-esteem you will also be contributing to the wellbeing of others, so don't hold back in your quest to be your best! This work is not always easy. Sometimes it *does* feel impossible to believe in yourself. But never doubt that you are progressing in your pursuit of self-esteem and know that all the love and support you need will always be available to you. And if you would like to get in touch with me or find out more about my life-coaching services just go to www.lyndafield.com or email me at lynda.field@btopenworld.com

I look forward to hearing from you.

With all my best wishes,

Lynda Field

References and Inspirational Books

Ban Breathnach, Sarah, *Simple Abundance*, Bantam Press, 1997

Chödrön, Pema, *No Time to Lose*, Shambhala Publications, 2005

Coelho, Paulo, *The Alchemist*, HarperCollins, 1999

Branden, Nathaniel, *The Six Pillars of Self-Esteem*, Bantam Press, 1995

Covey, Steven, *The Seven Habits of Highly Effective People*, Simon & Schuster UK Ltd, 1999

Field, Lynda, *Weekend Life Coach*, Vermilion, 2004

—— *Weekend Love Coach*, Vermilion, 2005

—— *Just Do it Now*, Vermilion, 2001

—— *Fast Track to Happiness*, Vermilion, 2007

Gawain, Shakti, *Creative Visualization*, Bantam New Age Books, 1983

Goleman, Daniel, *Healing Emotions*, Shambhala Publications, 1997

Hanh, Thich Nhat, *The Miracle of Mindfulness*, Rider, 1991

Hay, Louise, *You Can Heal Your Life*, Eden Grove Editions, 1988

HH Dalai Lama and Cutler, Howard C, *The Art of Happiness*, Hodder and Stoughton, 1999

Kamins, Marni and MacLeod, Janice, *The Break-up Repair Kit*, Conari Press, 2004

Ketchian, Lionel, www.happinessclub.com

Koran, Al, *Bring out the Magic in Your Mind*, A Thomas & Co., 1972

Kornfield, Jack, *A Path with Heart*, Rider, 1994

MacDonald, Lucy, *Learn to Be an Optimist*, Duncan Baird Publishers, 2004

Salzberg, Sharon, *Loving-Kindness*, Shambhala Publications, 1995

Satir, Virginia, *My Declaration of Self-Esteem*, freely available on the Internet

Seligman, Martin, *Authentic Happiness*, Nicholas Brealey Publishing Ltd, 2003

Sherfield, Robert M, *The Everything Self-Esteem Book*, Adams Media, 2004